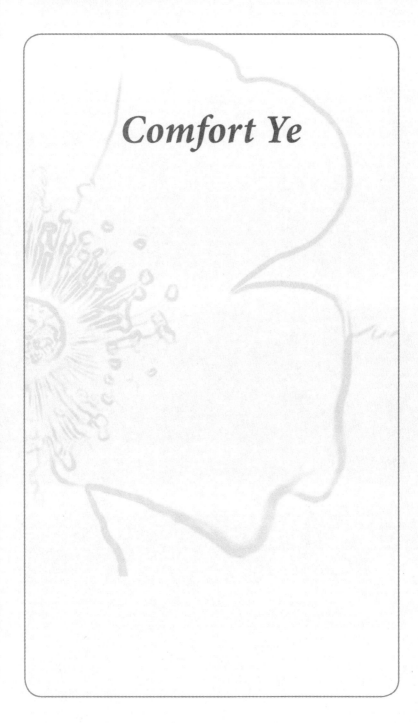

Comfort Ye

Comfort Ye

Finding Light
in Times of Darkness

Edited by
Richard H. Schmidt

Forward Movement
Cincinnati, Ohio

Cover and art: Albonetti Design
Book design: Carole Miller

©2007 Forward Movement
All rights reserved. Published 2007

ISBN 978-0-88028-303-8
Printed in Canada

Library of Congress Cataloging-in-Publication Data

Comfort ye : finding light in times of darkness / edited by Richard H.
Schmidt.
     p. cm.
  ISBN 978-0-88028-303-8 (alk. paper)
  1. Suffering--Religious aspects--Christianity. 2. Consolation. I.
Schmidt, Richard H., 1944-
   BV4909.C66 2007
   248.8'6--dc22

                                                                2007012983

FORWARD MOVEMENT
300 West Fourth Street, Cincinnati, Ohio 45202-2666 USA
1-800-543-1813
www.forwardmovement.org

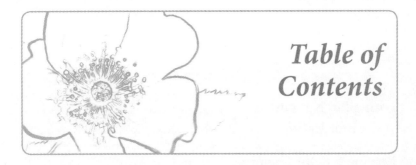

Table of Contents

Section II: Reflections

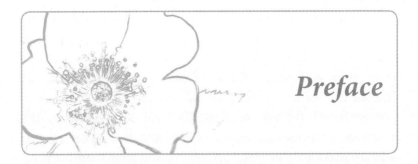

Preface

IMMEDIATELY following the terrorist attacks on September 11, 2001, the editors at Forward Movement asked several authors to contribute to a volume of meditations in response to the attacks. Within days, vignettes and reflections, each two or three paragraphs in length, began arriving at the Forward Movement office in Cincinnati. These pieces were quickly edited and the volume was rushed into production. It was available by October 1. One hundred thousand copies were sent at no charge to the impacted areas in New York and Arlington, Virginia, to families of victims and the parishes where they worshiped, and to whoever requested it. The response to the effort was voluminous and gratifying.

When hurricanes Katrina and Rita devastated the Gulf Coast in 2005, the editors again pondered how to respond. One possibility would have been to commission a similar volume for the victims of the storms. But it occurred to us that terrorist attacks and hurricanes, singularly horrific in their impact, are not the only tragedies, crises, and losses people face. Thoughtful souls ask the same kinds of questions following any loss—and the heartaches, longings, and sense of abandonment transcend any single event. We began to envision a volume we could make available to any person or group of persons experiencing a wrenching loss.

Again, we approached authors we knew could address these concerns. As the contributions began arriving in our office in the fall of 2005, we realized we had something more than a slender volume of brief meditations. We had invited the writers, if they felt so moved, to write pieces of greater length than those in the 2001 volume—and they did. Fourteen authors responded to our invitation. The result is a kaleidoscope of stories, insights, ruminations, and expressions of faith. The pieces in this volume are stunning in their variety. They have two things in common: each is undergirded by the author's Christian faith, and each addresses the hard questions head-on.

What are those hard questions? Not every piece in these pages speaks to every concern, but several questions recur, like leitmotifs in a symphony: How can I make sense out of a devastating loss? Where can I find support? Where is God in this event? Why does God allow it? How can I forgive those responsible?

These essays are divided into two sections. The division is not absolute; several essays could have been assigned to either section. The pieces in *Section I: Stories* arise out of a particular experience, usually that of the author. They are testimonies. Although they include reflective passages, often powerful ones, these are narrative essays and contain many personal references. Gregory A. Russell tells how he coped with the sudden death of his wife at the age of forty-seven. Robert Horine reflects on the murder of two close associates. David J. Bena writes of the challenge to his faith posed by the near death of an infant daughter. Kathryn Greene-McCreight describes her descent into mental illness and her recovery from it. Lee Krug writes about the healing which loving and understanding friends can generate. Edward J. Mills III relives the darkness and eventual redemption he experienced following the suicide of a young friend. Mary Wilson speaks of her faith as she comes to terms with amyotrophic lateral sclerosis (Lou Gehrig's disease).

The essays in *Section II: Reflections* are more general in character. Reference is made to particular events, but these pieces take a broader view. With fewer personal references, they directly address the theological, spiritual, and biblical issues posed by tragedy and loss. Carol McCrea discusses the importance of honestly facing and expressing how one feels. Francis H. Wade ponders how to pray for, rather than against, the perpetrators of evil. Desmond Tutu reflects on why God does not step in and prevent evil. John J. Thatamanil and Frederick W. Schmidt probe pertinent biblical texts, Thatamanil looking at the Book of Job and Schmidt at the experience of Jesus in the Garden of Gethsemane. Thomas L. Ehrich focuses on dealing with a loss resulting from a betrayal of trust. Rowan Williams affirms the Christian conviction that every individual person is beloved of God. And in a concluding essay, I answer a few questions while acknowledging that all answers are inadequate.

And that, perhaps, is the bottom line of this collection of essays: While those facing tragedy and loss may ask perplexing, painful, wrenching questions, it is not ultimately answers that they seek or need. It is love, relationship, faith. When losses lacerate our souls, it is hard to embrace love, relationship, and faith. But the essays in this volume show that it is possible to grow beyond the pain without discounting or forgetting it. However abandoned we may feel, we are not in fact abandoned, and God does not ultimately disappoint those who cry out to him.

Richard H. Schmidt
Cincinnati, Ohio
March 15, 2007

SECTION I

Stories

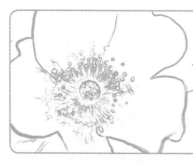

Pay Attention to the Nudges

Gregory A. Russell

SHE FIT perfectly in the crook of my left arm as we slept.

Jane, my wife of nineteen years, had just set up her office at our home and was working as the editorial director for Chalice Press, our church's publishing house in St. Louis. I was completing a long-term, interim assignment at North Christian Church (Disciples of Christ) in Columbus, Indiana. It was June of 2004; we had the world by the tail.

We had come to Columbus three years earlier for my assignment as interim pastor. That put us near Jane's family. During my time at North Christian, we held dueling interims, Jane serving as interim dean at St. Paul School of Theology in Kansas City. She commuted each week so she could be back in Columbus on the weekends with the church and the people she loved. When she finished her work at St. Paul's, she began at Chalice. It was her dream job, and best of all she could do the bulk of it over the Internet from home.

Our bliss was rudely interrupted June 24 when Jane died from a massive pulmonary embolism.

She awoke violently ill that awful Thursday morning. We rushed her to the hospital where physicians chased symptoms all day. By evening, when we had a firm diagnosis, it was too late for surgical intervention. Thankfully, we did not realize that at the time. We both thought she was going to make it right up to the very moment she died. She died the way she lived: full of hope, full of faith—and in a hurry. She stepped out of this life and into the next at 10:45 p.m.; she was forty-seven. I staggered home under a moon as full and bright as any I ever had seen.

On Monday, we held a celebration of her life at the church. Her ashes are buried in the memorial garden there.

The Sunday after, the congregation called its new senior minister. He would arrive in two months. It was the moment toward which we had worked and prayed for three years—a time for rejoicing. Yet at the same time, I had new appreciation for the words, "All dressed up with nowhere to go."

Over the next two months I did all those things I had counseled people not to do during twenty-five years of ministry: I changed jobs, I moved, I changed support systems. I was in conversation with a fine church about a pastoral position.

Meanwhile, I had an interim to finish. One of the things I needed to do with the good folks at the church was talk openly about the enormous changes buffeting us all. We needed to ask: *Where is God in the midst of all this? Can we still sense God's presence somehow?* It was not my question alone; we were all asking it. I hoped to assure them that I still felt God's presence. In my most honest moments, I had to admit I needed to say it out loud to assure myself as well.

To my surprise I began to sense God primarily in the small things of life, things we often take for granted or fail to notice. I wanted to invite them to experience God there, too. I came to the conclusion these little points of grace come to us unbidden and that if we pay attention, occasionally we recognize them.

That is still my conviction. There is a good deal more going on among us, within us, and around us than we are able to know, let alone articulate. Yet we all seem to have been schooled in rational and empirical thought as the only way to relate to the world. Consequently, we often ignore or fail to see the subtle intimations of the connection to the greater One who influences our lives. William Blake describes it this way:

> To see a world in a grain of sand
> and a heaven in a wild flower,
> Hold infinity in the palm of your hand
> and eternity in an hour.*

This is not some sort of modernist, New Age idea; the Bible is full of examples, from Moses encountering God "in the thick darkness" at Sinai (Exodus 20:21), to Isaiah murmuring, "Truly, thou art a God who hidest thyself" (Isaiah 45:15), to Elijah discerning God in "a still, small voice" after having searched in all the big events of his day (1 Kings 19:12), to Paul's eloquent description of the search as "feeling after and finding God" (Acts 17:27). Our most honest and heartfelt efforts to describe these encounters with the divine render us speechless. Yet they need not if we pay attention and reflect on them.

The pieces of my story allow you to stitch them together in whatever pattern makes sense to you. After all, this is your story, too—or will be; none of us is exempt. These are scenes from a couple of weeks on either side of Jane's death.

                                   & & &

---

* "Auguries of Innocence," William Blake (1757-1827).

Scene One: Our eldest niece, Katherine, was nine-and-a-half (the half being very important at this age) and was rereading the books in the Harry Potter series. The Tuesday before Jane died, Katherine and her mother stopped by the library to pick up the next book in the series. Alas, no copies were on the shelf, so they filled out a request slip, and the librarian behind the desk said, "We'll call you when one comes in." And indeed they did. They called that afternoon about 1:30, and Katherine had the book she wanted. It was a huge help to her that difficult weekend as all the adults descended on her house, attending to a flurry of details: clearing schedules, tracking down speakers, organizing music, choosing readings. Katherine immersed herself in her book as the chaos of mourning swirled about her. Harry Potter and his friends provided immense comfort for her.

What we came to realize as the weekend unfolded was that she had that particular book because Jane's mother, Helen, had joined us for lunch that Tuesday. We chose a restaurant downtown, and on the way out the door, Jane said, "Oh, wait; if we are going that direction, I have this book that needs to go back to the library."

The book she retuned was—of course—the next book in the Harry Potter series, the one which Katherine had requested only hours earlier. Jane returned it right after lunch, the library called Katherine, and her mom drove her into town to pick up the very copy of the book that Aunt Jane had just brought in. And upon realizing this, my offhand thought was, *Well, Jane always knew just what we needed.* But it was a nudge—a small one, granted—but a nudge nonetheless.

Pay attention to the nudges.

      & *&* *&*

Scene Two: The evening before we gathered in North Church to celebrate Jane's life, I had wrestled all night with the idea of assembling tangible symbols to represent her life's work. Rick Spleth, who was to preach at the service, suggested I find a way to tell her life's story symbolically. To do that, I chose her open laptop computer with a pile of manuscripts in the process of being edited on the left and her finished books on the right. I hoped to indicate the transition from thought to editing to finished product. Jane's mentor at seminary once had told her, "Your real gift is taking complex theological discourse and breaking it down into components that are accessible to others." She took his counsel to heart and spent the balance of her life doing that very thing as preacher, educator, author, and editor.

I had no qualms about displaying the books she herself had written, but wondered about displaying those she only had edited. Would that be bragging too much? She had edited twenty volumes in just the few months she had worked for Chalice Press. I wrestled all night with the decision, and in the morning arose with a certainty that said, "Oh, for heaven's sake, give the woman her due." So I went into the study and was packing up her "godchildren," as she called them, the books she inherited in progress and saw to completion.

Having packed them up, along with a couple of book-ends and her ever-present University of Chicago coffee mug, my eye drifted over to a shelf where there were books Jane had read recently for her own enjoyment. Idly, I pulled one out—a book I never had seen before—and opened it.

Jane was a confirmed underliner, so I had no trouble telling what had caught her eye and sparked her interest. On the right-hand page of the open book, this is the sentence she had underlined: "Through the redeeming power of memory, even the saddest things can become, once we have made peace with them, a source of wisdom and strength for the journey that still lies ahead." *

I know, I know: it was just random chance; at least that's what we're taught to think. But I couldn't help wondering why this particular sentence on this particular page in this particular book on this particular day. It drove me to my knees as my words came back to me: *She always knew just what we needed*...Evidently she still did.

Pay attention to the nudges.

& & &

Scene Three: A few weeks prior to Jane's death, knowing North Church was close to calling their new senior minister, Rick Spleth said he thought I should take a look at a downstate church. I had suggested the possibility to Jane, but she was not keen on it. She wanted to be near her family in Columbus and live in our condo, which we had just renovated. And who could blame her? We talked it over. "No dice." I called Rick and said, "Thanks, but no thanks." The day of her memorial service, however, I told him I was ready to reconsider. He was already one step ahead of me, and we arranged a hurried, under-the-radar-visit.

Ever since Rick had first mentioned this church to me, I'd had a recurring vision—I simply can't describe it any other way—a vision of a bungalow, an Arts and Crafts movement house from the 1920s. With perfect clarity I saw the porch with substantial columns all the way across the front, a porch swing at one end, a *porte cochere* across the driveway, and a detached garage at the back of the lot. I just could not get the picture of this place out of my mind! I had to

---

* Peter S. Hawkins quoting Frederick Buechner in *Listening for God.* Paula J. Carlson and Peter S. Hawkins, eds. (Minneapolis: Augsburg Fortress, 1994), p. 39.

admit this was a lot more specific than any vision I'd ever heard of, let alone experienced.

As we arrived in town and drove down Main Street toward the church, I looked over to see the very house I'd been imagining. There was no mistaking it. "Rick, stop the car," I shouted. "There's my house!" He pulled over to the curb and stopped while I tried to remember how to breathe and while I told him about seeing this house so clearly in my mind's eye.

This is a town my parents and I used to pass through when I was a child on the way to see my aunt and her family. Obviously I had to be *remembering* this house rather than *imagining* it. So I said that to Rick, who had made a U-turn in the street and pulled up in front of the cottage.

Rick nodded and smiled indulgently. And then he said, "Well, Greg, that explains seeing the house so clearly in your mind's eye. What it doesn't explain, though, is the 'For Sale' sign here in the front yard."

"Okay, Rick," I said, "is this creeping you out? It's creeping me out!"

And he replied, "No, actually, I'm okay with all this."

I decided it was immaterial whether or not I wound up with that particular house. The way I chose to read this experience was that I was meant to have a very serious conversation with the folks from this church. And so I did. They invited me to become their pastor, which I did the following January.

Pay attention to the nudges.

I can't help but remember the time Jane and I visited Portugal in the spring of 2000. We went to the little town of Sagres, the southwesternmost spit of land on the continent of Europe. Here land ends. This is where Prince Henry the Navigator had his famous sailing school. We climbed up inside the old lighthouse and looked out into the vastness of the black Atlantic Ocean, that place where on ancient maps they used to print, "Beyond here there be dragons," complete with sketches.

So confident were they of their assessment that they had placed boulders into the side of the cliff to make gigantic letters which you could read from a passing ship, letters which spelled out *Ne Plus Ultra*—No More Beyond.

But there *was* more beyond. And when word reached them of Columbus's successful voyage and return, they raced to the cliff and tore out the boulders that formed the word "Ne" so that it now read *Plus Ultra*—More Beyond.

More beyond; there is more beyond. And while I have not yet seen it with my own eyes, it is as real to me as any new world.

Elizabeth Barrett Browning has it right:

> *Earth's crammed with heaven,*
> *And every common bush afire with God;*
> *And only he who sees takes off his shoes—*
> *The rest sit round it and pluck blackberries.**

I confess to having plucked more than my share of blackberries. But every once in awhile, I manage to see—and I take off my shoes.

Pay attention to the nudges.

---

* Elizabeth Barrett Browning, *Aurora Leigh* (Book VII, Line 820).

Anatomy of Forgiveness

Robert Horine

IN MEMORY the afternoon was sunny and warm. The office was closing for the day. Exiting the building on Cincinnati's Sycamore Street, I turned left and headed for the parking garage a short block away across Fourth Street. Ahead of me were Joan and Michelle, mother and daughter, who worked in our office.

As they prepared to cross Fourth, a car sped by and skidded to a halt just beyond the intersection. When the women reached the other side they turned left toward the garage's Fourth Street entrance. I was not quite across the street when the car suddenly backed around the corner onto Fourth, so recklessly that I had to jump out of the way. I yelled something at the driver, but he paid me no attention, sped back around onto Sycamore, and raced down the hill toward Third. That was the last I saw of him that day.

I entered the garage by the Sycamore entrance and stepped onto an elevator. At the third level Joan and Michelle got on. I said, "Did you see that guy? He almost hit me!" Michelle showed me a small canister in her hand and said, "I've got my Mace."

We left the elevator on the same floor and said something like, "See you tomorrow." It was the last time we saw each other. A few minutes after they left the garage they were dead. The man in the speeding car was Michelle's estranged boyfriend. He chased them, caught up with them in a parking lot a few blocks away, and in front of horrified witnesses shot them to death. A passing off-duty policeman came upon the scene and a gun battle ensued. Though severely wounded—he would lose an arm—the killer didn't stop firing until he was physically unable to reload.

I learned about the murders when I arrived at the office the next morning. My boss said I should tell the police what I had seen, and I did. Later the prosecutor's office interviewed me. I had not been closer to Joan and Michelle than to others in the office, but I had lived with them in the last moments of their lives. Again and again I replayed that afternoon, thinking that if I had known their danger I could have done something, maybe spirited them away in my car.

Though I said I was okay, a co-worker knew I wasn't, and after much persuasion on her part I agreed to talk with a police chaplain. I am to this day amazed at what came out of me in that interview—the rage, words damning a man to hell. The chaplain was good at his job: first deal with the emotions, then work on forgiving.

The trial was in winter; there was snow the day I testified, and in keeping with the season I coolly told what I knew. This was a capital crime and I was helping send a man to death row. He was found guilty and so sentenced, but as in most such cases, delays have kept him alive. It's not fair.

At a memorial service at Auschwitz in 1995, Holocaust survivor, author, and teacher Elie Wiesel, winner of a Nobel Peace Prize, said this prayer: "God of forgiveness, do not forgive those who created this place. God of mercy, have no mercy on those who killed Jewish children here."

I understand his prayer, though I mustn't pray such a thing. Jesus didn't make it easy for Christians. How often must I forgive the person who sins against me? As many as seven times? No, Jesus said, not seven times, but seventy times seven—every time. In the Lord's Prayer he gave us this petition: "Forgive us our sins as we forgive those who sin against us." As he was dying he forgave his executioners.

Forgiveness is not a matter of feelings, but of will. Often it means getting on your knees, figuratively or literally, and talking with God about your problem—for it is *your* problem—until it's resolved. With enough practice, even feelings change over time.

It also means talking with God about the offender. What shall I pray, that he be released from prison to try again for a good life? Not so fast, for God is a God of justice as well as of mercy and our actions have necessary consequences. And anyway, I don't want justice so much as I want vengeance. Shall I pray that he repents before he is executed or dies in prison? That seems to be the right thing, but then I remember him sitting in the courtroom, cool and composed, his lawyer suggesting Joan and Michelle brought it on themselves. I remember the photos of their bodies, hardly recognizable.

What shall I pray? The best I can do is to offer him up: "Here he is, God. Break his heart and have mercy on him." And I have to pray the same for myself; I have to let the hunger for vengeance go.

To be unforgiving is to live in a dangerous place. I once read the unsettling statement that you can love God only as much as you love your worst enemy.

It is, sometimes, a very hard thing to forgive. But it's necessary for the health of one's soul. Many years later I'm still working on forgiving the killer of my friends. I'm bound to do it, feelings aside, because I have promised to follow Jesus, and as the spiritual song puts it, "no turning back, no turning back."

Yea, Though I Walk Through the Valley

David J. Bena

"CHU LAI TOWER, Marine Delta-Tango-Zero-Six is twenty miles north for landing," I called as we descended through ten thousand feet. My pilot and I were returning from a bombing mission in North Vietnam. I had had trouble concentrating on this particular mission. Just before we launched, I had been notified that my wife had given birth to our first child. The message got to me a whopping four days after Laurel was born. I was pumped up with pride and joy. I thought about it the whole mission and decided that when we landed I would rush over to the ham radio shack and call Mary Ellen.

We landed and caught some breakfast. Then I headed to the radio shack to make the call. The line was long and the weather hot. One hundred marines were lined up so that, one at a time, each could make a two-minute call home. I figured it would take five hours before I got to the front of the line—if the radio waves cooperated. Five hours waiting to call my wife in the middle of her night to congratulate her for a job well done. Five hours waiting in the 110-degree sun. Was it worth it? You bet it was.

The five hours ticked by, and finally it was my turn. The good-hearted ham operator in the States placed the collect call to Mary Ellen.

"Hello?" said a sleepy voice.

"Collect call for Mary Ellen Bena from David Bena. Will you accept the charges?"

"Yes!" came the rapid reply. "Dave, it is so good to hear from you!"

"Congratulations on having Laurel. You did good!" I said flippantly.

"Dave, Laurel is in trouble. We had to take her back to the hospital. Can you come home?"

I hesitated. "I'm kind of in the middle of a war here. Is her condition serious?"

"Yes. She's been having seizures. Please come home!"

"I'll try" was all I could say. "I'll try to figure out how to come home. I love you."

"I love you, too. Please pray for us."

Suddenly my life was turned upside down. We had recently joined a church, and I was becoming active in my faith. Here, in Vietnam, I was involved in a Bible study group where we were discussing God's involvement in our lives. I had smugly begun to believe the "health and wealth" concept of God—if you commit your life to God, he will take care of you, protect you, and grant what you ask. I had already flown ninety bombing missions and had not been shot down—obviously God was protecting me. So when I heard that my newborn daughter was threatened with death in infancy, I was thrown for a loop. Where was God in this? Why was he allowing this to happen when I was so far away from home? Doubts and fears began to beat at me, like hard rain against a windowpane.

Back at squadron headquarters, I found my pilot and summarized Mary Ellen's call. Since he was ten years older than me, I figured he might have a solution to my problem.

"You need emergency leave, Dave," Bill explained. "And to get it, you need a doctor's request that you go home. Let's go down to the Red Cross office and see if they can send a message to Bethesda Naval Hospital asking for clarification." We did that, and then the wait began.

While I waited I continued to fly missions. In between, I prayed for understanding and talked with my Bible study friends. We began to search the scriptures. "God does not purposely afflict his loved ones," we read in Lamentations 3:33. That caught my attention. I couldn't believe God would purposely afflict my infant daughter, and this passage seemed to bear that out. But part of me was wondering whether God might be punishing me for dropping bombs on people. Would God do that? So I had to do some studying and thinking about that. I realized God does not operate that way. My participation in the war was part of my Christian commitment to my country. Sometimes controlled force has to be applied to contain overt evil when negotiations bring no resolution. That's what war is. As a surgeon sometimes has to cut into good tissue to remove a cancerous tumor, sometimes nations have to do such international surgery to remove evil from being a threat to world peace. I understood all that, and finally came to the conclusion that my daughter's illness was not the result of my part in the war.

Maybe it's just chance, I reasoned, just the odds. Some people get sick and die. It might be happening to her. Just happenstance! At first, that sounded logical to me. But where is God if this is just a random world? The scriptures showed God to be active in the lives of his people. So where was he now? Tired? "Where are you, God?" I yelled at him. "I insist that you heal my daughter now!"

Three days later, the Red Cross message arrived: "Neonatal seizures; condition guarded; request service member's presence with his family ASAP." And written by a doctor!

I grabbed the message and ran across the field to the squadron commander's office. After he read it carefully, he called the administrative officer. "Cut emergency leave orders for Captain Bena immediately. Get him a high transportation priority number to Travis Air Force Base." Then to me, he said sympathetically, "Dave, I hope your daughter makes it. I'll pray for her."

I left Chu Lai that afternoon in a helicopter, and by that night I was on a big C-141 cargo jet heading home. As I traveled, I prayed and read the Bible. I happened upon the Book of Job. As I read it, I recognized myself in Job. My child was possibly dying right then, or maybe even was dead. I could find no reason for it, nor could I find any empirical evidence that God would do anything about it. I began to despair as Job had done. This was, I thought, just like Job. As I read on, one thing caught my attention about Job and his relationship with God. For most of the book, every philosophy about suffering was investigated, with no logical conclusion. In the end, God told Job that he was just going to have to trust him. And in the end, Job did just that. Inner peace resulted. So I began to think more about my situation. All this time I had been demanding answers, threatening God, bargaining with him, denying his involvement, demanding his involvement. And all that did was bring on more anxiety. Maybe, I thought, I should just do all I can to help my wife through the crisis and trust God with the rest. Philippians 4:6-7 came to mind: "Have no anxiety about anything, but in everything by prayer and supplication with thanksgiving make your requests known to God. And the peace of God, which passes all understanding, will keep your hearts and your minds in Christ Jesus."

Somewhere over Japan, I decided to live into the Philippians passage. I said quietly, "O Lord, you love Laurel more than I'll ever be able to. So I give her completely over to you, whether she lives or dies. I thank you for her, whether it be for a day or a lifetime. I trustfully place her and this situation totally in your hands." The prayer ended, and I fell into a peaceful sleep.

The rest of the trip was uneventful. I arrived home the next day, in time to accompany my wife to the hospital where our little daughter was released into our care. She had made it. And I had a bonus week to get to know her before I went back to the war.

Today she is thirty-seven years old, beautiful, in good health, and a mother. Sometimes I wonder what would have happened to my faith if I had gotten home to find a weeping wife and a dead daughter. I honestly cannot answer that. But I can say that since that time, I have had a stronger faith and trust in God, whether the outcome is good or bad. I have gone through near-death in war, my wife's serious illness, family crises, a roller coaster in my ministry, the death of loved ones, a totally destroyed car, a house terribly damaged by a hurricane, and physical problems. Although I never knew what the outcome of any of those events would be, I tried to live Philippians 4:6-7. God strengthened me.

And so to you, I quote from the words of Jesus: "I have said this to you, that in me you may have peace. In the world you have tribulation; but be of good cheer. I have overcome the world" (John 16:33).

The Light Shines in the Darkness

Kathryn Greene-McCreight

THE MENTALLY ILL are handicapped people against whom it still seems socially acceptable to hold prejudice, to make jokes, and to avoid on the streets. Despite media personalities like Jane Pauley, Brooke Shields, and Kay Redfield Jamison, all of whom have experienced either depression and/or mania, this seems to be as true in the Christian communities as in the secular world. Why is this? I suggest that people in general, despite the recent media attention to mental illness, still fear the mentally ill. Fear comes from the stigma of mental illness, and stigma in turn is fed by the fear.

There is also a false assumption among some Christians that the Christian life should always be easy, and that anyone who is mentally ill is not truly faithful, not really Christian enough. Either that or their religiousness is part of their mental problem. On top of this, mental illness is hard to accept because the larger problem of suffering in general is so hard to grasp. C. S. Lewis suggests in *The Problem of Pain* that suffering is uniquely difficult for the Christian, for the one who believes in a "good" God. If there were no good God to factor into the equation, suffering would be not only painful but ultimately meaningless, because it would be random.

For the Christian, then, who believes in the crucified and risen Messiah, suffering is meaningful. It is meaningful because of Jesus, the one in whose suffering we participate. This is not to suggest, of course, that suffering will be pleasant, nor that it is to be sought. Rather, in the personal suffering of the Christian, one finds a parallel to Christ's suffering, which gathers up our tears, calms our sorrows, and points us toward his resurrection. So I have found my own suffering with mental illness to be significant in my life before God, and hope that by sharing part of my story I may help those who have trouble accepting mental illness, either their own or that of others.

It has been estimated that 2.8 percent of the adult population—roughly eight million people—have experienced or are now experiencing severe and persistent mental illness. Add to that the mentally ill homeless, the incarcerated mentally ill, and children with psychological problems, and we can conclude that over 20 million Americans are directly affected by persistent and serious forms of mental illness. Individuals with serious mental illness are everywhere among us.

How does one become mentally ill? There are many theories, but the reigning ones suggest that it is a combination of nature and nurture; that is, one's brain biology or genetic makeup combines with the stresses and traumas of one's life. This means that the way to combat mental illness is usually to combine psychotherapeutic approaches to deal with traumas and medical approaches to deal with brain biology.

Genetics exerts a strong influence in my own case, but so does life stress. Mental illness runs in my family. My brother and father both suffer from depression. A first cousin made an attempt on his life. A great-grandfather was an alcoholic, and sometimes alcoholics are mentally ill folk who use alcohol to self-medicate. From the family tree there are stories of other eccentrics.

I have a chronic disease, the brain disorder which used to be called manic-depression, now less offensively called bipolar disorder. However one tries to soften the blow of the diagnosis, bipolar disorder is still a major mental illness.

Mental illnesses affect people differently. Some can't get out of bed, some sleep too much, some can't sleep. Some eat too much, some can't bring themselves to eat. The symptoms are not the diseases. And the diseases are not like cancers which can be cut out of the body. The whole mind and body are afflicted.

I am not necessarily sad when I am depressed. I am not necessarily "down." I do have a gnawing, overwhelming sense of grief, with no identifiable cause. I grieve my loved ones as though they were dead, contemplating what their funerals would be like. I feel completely alone; darkness is my only companion. I feel as if I am walking barefoot on broken glass. When one steps on broken glass, the weight of one's body grinds the glass in further with every movement. The weight of my very existence grinds the shards of grief deeper into my soul. When I am depressed, every thought, every breath, every conscious moment hurts.

So what do I do? I try to distract myself. Enduring an episode of depression requires that I expend huge amounts of energy just to distract myself, just to do the bare minimum. My work, when I can by sheer force of will overcome the depression enough to engage in work, is solace. Prayer, when I can climb out of the hole depression throws me into, helps momentarily. Of course, theologically speaking, I know it helps more than momentarily, but that is not the way it feels. Reading scripture, especially the lament psalms, is a great comfort. Sleeping, while I am sleeping, if I can sleep, helps as an escape. Tasks, busy-ness, gardening, tidying up: distraction. Mustn't think, mustn't be conscious, mustn't reflect. This escape from consciousness is what is at the heart of suicidal energy. It is *not* necessarily wanting to hurt the self. It is simply wanting *not to hurt*. And when I am depressed, it seems that the only way not to hurt is to cease being a center of consciousness. While God certainly can pick up the pieces and put them together in a new way, this can only happen if the depressed person makes it through to see life again. However, during the freefall of depression such a possibility seems unimaginable.

Just as depression is more than sadness, mania is more than speeding mentally, euphoria, and creative genius. The sick individual cannot simply shrug it off or pull out of it. My brain tingles and sparkles, I soar, all things connect, I am at one with all creation, and then within a second everything snaps out of euphoria into sheer panic and utter paranoia. I don't know where I am, or how I got there, or even what "home" is like or how I will return.

My first depressive episode as an adult occurred after my second child was born in 1992. Postpartum depression is not pretty. It is the number one complication of childbirth. We have all heard about women who destroy their own children while depressed soon after giving birth. Every instinct in the mother usually pushes toward preserving the life of the child. Most mothers would give their own lives to protect their babies. But in a postpartum depression, reality is so bent that that instinct is blocked. Severe sleep deprivation alone could make one depressed and hallucinatory. On top of that the rigors of infant care are enough to push anyone to her limit, and in addition the new mother has a rush of hormones playing havoc with body and brain. Perfectly good mothers have had their confidence shaken by the thoughts and feelings they endure in postpartum depression.

Postpartum depression generally goes away. I, however, continued to experience excruciating depression in waves throughout the next five years. Then, during the Christmas holidays when my youngest was five years old, I experienced my first manic period. Both the diagnosis and the medical regimen became more complicated. A diagnosis of depression is one thing, but bipolar disorder does not appear to "go away." I must think of myself as having a chronic illness, like diabetes, which I will have to manage the rest of my life. I have read that 10 percent of cases of bipolar disorder are terminal. Particularly in mismanaged cases, depression can lead to suicide and mania can lead to accidental death. My psychiatrist tells me that if I ever go off of my medication, in cases like mine the relapse rate is near 100 percent.

I have suffered much from mental illness, yet there are certainly those who have suffered more, who have lost their families and friends from mental illness. I do not claim any corner on the market of suffering from mental illness. But I do know that without my trust in my God who raises the dead, and without the support of my family, and prayer, I could have been one of the 10 percent who die.

But God lifted me out of the mire. "A threefold cord is not quickly broken" (Ecclesiastes 4:12). With prayer, medicine, and therapy, God has wrought healing in my soul, a resurrection from my own psychological death. Prayer was especially healing for me, even when I could not feel God's presence. I strapped myself to the prayers of tradition, those of the ancients, the great saints, and those of the saints in my parish and family. To know I was being prayed for was a great comfort, and I believe I would not have been healed as soon but for the prayers of others and my own feeble groanings to the Lord.

I learned many lessons from my illnesses and my healing. I learned anew what compassion truly is. I look now at the homeless in a completely different light. Whereas before, I admit, I feared them, now I see myself in their illnesses and sufferings. I know that if it were not for the love and fidelity of my family, I could be homeless. I have learned the power of the Holy Spirit to help me persevere in the faith of Christ even when I cannot feel it. I have learned that our feelings in our life of faith are often not as important as I once thought. Our life before God is not governed by our moods and feelings but by the very faithfulness of God. I have learned the power of memory in the life of faith. When we cannot feel the love of God, we must remember it.

Memory is a great power in healing, a gift of the grace of God. I also learned that some mental illness can be controlled, that it is not simply a life sentence. I have learned so much from my illness that I can see it as, in some respects, a mercy. Now I can say with the evangelist, "The light shines in the darkness, and the darkness cannot overcome it" (John 1:5).

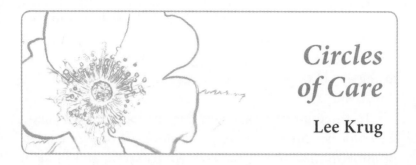

Circles of Care

Lee Krug

I WATCH their eyes as they return from communion. Many are composed; a few are teary; some are thoughtful; a few look happy. For many years, as a clergy wife and a psychotherapist, I have been aware of what lies in their souls. They have confided in me the secrets of their hearts, and at times I marvel that they are able still to be on their feet and in the congregation.

When tragedies happen on a large scale—tsunamis, earthquakes, floods, and other natural disasters—the entire world pays attention. If there is a terrorist attack, a huge plane crash, the explosion of a space shuttle, the media brings us minute details, interviews, and pictures. At times the attention seems almost intrusive. Community resources are available, although they sometimes falter. The horrors of every "big event" filter down to a multitude of individual or family tragedies. Whatever our faith may be, we are called to encircle the people in crisis, to be with them in their suffering, and to offer them hope for their futures.

We received a call one morning from a parishioner and friend. His seventeen-year-old daughter had pulled out of the driveway in their car on her way to school, and was hit broadside by a school bus. She was still alive at a nearby hospital, where physicians were frantically trying to reduce the swelling in her brain. Before nightfall she was dead. Her father, Paul, was distraught. I felt punched in the belly as if a horse had kicked me. We had young children. The idea of losing one of them was unthinkable. Yet it had happened to our friend.

In the following two days Paul had created a bulletin cover for her funeral service. The chief feature was a large, brightly shining sun. It represented her spirit, and to me it also symbolized the circle of care that had formed around Paul. People held him in their arms and wept with him. We reminisced about his daughter. We sat in silence with him. We did not try to tell him we understood what he was feeling, because we didn't. None of us had lost a child. We did not tell him that God wanted her to be in heaven with him. That would be a beastly kind of God. We did not tell him to feel glad that she would have no more suffering. In the ups and downs of life we all have suffering, and we accept it as a price for being alive. Both she and her father would have preferred it that way. We did not even tell him that God was with him in his suffering, although we did believe that.

The fact was that nothing we could say would make any difference. What mattered was that we were there, and continued to be there for a long time, as he was ready to fall into the pit. (He did not.) We were people who believed that the Holy Spirit was in the midst of us, giving us the strength to help our friend and ourselves survive tragedy.

Years later when we faced a crisis, that dear man came round every week with a six-pack of beer, and just sat with us. We may have chit-chatted, but he offered no solutions. He was not there as a problem solver; he was present as a part of our circle of care, and the presence of God. We never forgot it.

Another call came. I was older then, and presumably more experienced in dealing with tragedy. Forget that. Tragedy still punches you in the stomach. The caller was a relative telling us what had just happened to a young family in our parish. The mother had set forth in their car with their four-year-old daughter and two-year-old son, on a dark icy night. She had collided head-on with a snow plow whose massive front tore into her car. She and the little girl were killed. The toddler boy was taken to the hospital, where he remained for several months. He was blinded in the accident. Could anyone describe the state of mind and spirit of the father? I cannot. But their wide circle of family and friends embraced around him and his son. Did anybody dare tell him that his wife and daughter were not really lost? I don't think so. They were gone and he had to recognize that truth. One of the scenes I remember most vividly happened after the bodies were cremated. A number of us sat with the father in a circle and passed around the container with the ashes. Each of us held it a minute and felt the weight of the spirits now gone from us. How else can God reach us except through one another?

Our present church has a shelter for homeless people. Their stories could break your heart. Lena tells me about the daughter she gave up at birth for adoption because she could not care for her. The adoptive family keeps in touch with Lena and sends her notes and pictures, which she proudly shows me. Her daughter is now six years old. She hopes that when the child is eighteen, there can be a meeting.

The homeless form their own circle of care. They become family and community to one another. Last year a homeless woman was found dead under a truck. A church service was held for her in a special room. Her sleeping bag was laid out in front of a makeshift altar. Flowers were provided so that each person could lay one on her sleeping bag. Homeless people spoke about her, including a man who had been in love with her. God is surely in the midst of these folks who look out for each other and make their circles of care in places the world has forgotten.

Perhaps the most difficult losses are those which cannot be revealed to the world. A marriage is devastated by an affair. Only a priest or a therapist may be entrusted with the couple's loss and sorrow. You can see it in their eyes when they come down from communion. One or two people can hold that couple in a small but powerful circle of care. The unspeakable wounds we suffer, and give, may begin to heal when we share them with someone outside the situation. Whatever name your God may have, he or she needs people to be channels of grace for the Spirit of life and love to enter the scene.

Some churches have times of sharing in the middle of the service. People come to the front to speak of their sorrows, concerns, and joys. A young man stands up and says tearfully that he has just lost his job, and he is worried and frightened. A woman talks about her elderly mother who cannot adjust to living in a nursing home, and the guilt she feels for placing her there. An older man shares his crisis about an ethical issue in the company of which he is the CEO. A couple with an autistic child asks our prayers that they will find the right school for her. A woman manages to choke out that she has been diagnosed with cancer. All these people are speaking of crisis and loss. They are not asking the rest of us to take on their problems. They are wanting us, as part of their faith community, to support them with prayers and to witness that God cares about them.

Sorrows never really go away, but they can be transformed. When I was young, an old lady in our parish told me that the world expected her to be stoic about the death of her husband of more than fifty years. After all, they had had so many years together, she should feel satisfied. She said, "It matters how long you have been married because in a good marriage it only makes you want more." As she lived with her grief, she also continued to invite us and other friends to the lighting of her Christmas tree with real candles, and a bucket of water nearby. She kept faith with the traditions she and her husband had shared.

Memory of loss can strike us at unexpected moments. My mother died eight years ago. Recently I was in a variety store and saw a box of Coty face powder. I had not seen this brand for many years and thought it was no longer manufactured. It was the powder my mother always used. I bought a box, and when I opened it, the aroma was just the same, bringing tears to my eyes. She was a beautiful Southern lady, a flirt, and a devout believer in the Bible, Jesus, and the world to come. I am comforted to think the smell of that face powder rose like incense and made her smile wherever she is in God's kingdom.

Our visible world is supported by an invisible world with many resources and treasures. The boundaries are permeable. We can reach the help we need if we are open to God's presence in the most terrible moments of grief and tragedy.

Nothing bad that happens is the will of God. We can drive ourselves crazy with questions about why a good God lets such things befall us, and doesn't stop them. If we reasoned our way to an answer, would it do us any good? Loss is still loss, and I can't think of any good reason that would be a comfort. As a professional counselor I find that most people start with "Why?" or "Why me?" and move on to "How can I live through this?" Many express anger toward God, and I tell them that God is tough enough to take their anger and tender enough to help them stop blaming.

In most cases of loss, there is blame: "the terrorists" (September 11), "slow response from government agencies" (Katrina, tsunamis, earthquakes), "business" (job loss), "a scheming man/woman" (marriage break-up), "prejudice" (my child didn't get into that favored college), and so on. While there may sometimes be truth in blame, we need to free ourselves from its bondage in order to allow the people of God to hold us. Whatever evil or human error is responsible, we cannot go backwards, unravel it, and weave it a different way. "In order to get from what was to what will be, you must go through what is," said Ashleigh Brilliant.[*]

Recently I received a brochure for a training program with a large headline: "If time doesn't heal a broken heart, what does?" It was followed by "In four days we teach you what time cannot." This may be a helpful seminar, but could I really learn the secrets of healing, grief, and loss in four days? It is a long road.

Walk that long road with your faith community. Believe that they are healers, these ordinary people who are in touch with God in the invisible worlds within us and outside us. If you have suffered a terrible loss, your life will never be the same. You may want to withdraw and protect yourself, and you may be totally distraught. How you react to that loss determines whether you will survive as a changed person with the capacity to embrace life again. Your

---

[*] Ashleigh Brilliant, *I Have Abandoned My Search for Truth, and Am Now Looking for a Good Fantasy* (Santa Barbara: Woodbridge Press, 1981).

reaction may depend on how much you entrust yourself to God's circle of care.

I once attended a seminar in which members of the group were asked, one by one, to jump off a high table into the arms of all the others, who interlaced arms to catch them. For me, it was a very scary exercise. It was literally a leap of faith! When I screwed up my courage and jumped, I was caught and supported by the group. I had trusted their circle of care. And, in turn, I gave that support to others. This was not an assignment in the midst of crisis or tragedy, but was meant to teach us to trust one another in the happenings of life.

If we ask, "What next, God?" the answer may be, "Who knows? But I have sent you other people so you will know I'm traveling that road with you."

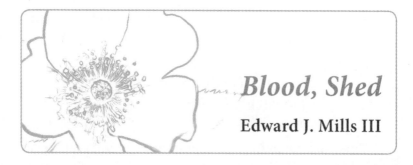

Blood, Shed

Edward J. Mills III

THIS ESSAY is about tragedy and accidental redemption. It tells of a savage shedding of blood, and the loss of hope that it caused. It also tells of a redemption that comes from another shedding of blood. I have pondered my reasons for writing this story. Of some of them I am still unsure. I do know that I am writing it for myself.

The word "redemption" is a mystifying word for many. Here it simply means that in a very painful experience I finally found peace, and began to understand. I use the religious word "redemption" because I believe God had a hand in my "accidental" redemption.

I begin with the end of the story and the "accident" that was the catalyst for my healing.

Many years ago I served as priest of a small, rural Episcopal church. The Episcopal Church is catholic in many ways. The central act of worship for us is the eucharist, what many people call communion. We believe that when the priest and people offer bread and wine to God in thanksgiving and prayer that the bread and wine become the body and blood of the risen Christ. We have never painted ourselves into a corner by trying to say how this happens. We simply proclaim that we have experienced this reality. It is experienced at the level of sign and symbol, of dream and vision. Words ascribed to Queen Elizabeth I best sum it up:

He (Christ) was the Word that spake it:
He took the bread and brake it;
And what that word did make it,
I do believe and take it.

This understanding of communion is integral to my story. One Sunday as we moved through the eucharist I found myself administering not just the bread of communion but also the chalice. This had never happened before. A lay person licensed by the bishop normally served the cup, following me. This particular Sunday the lay person assigned did not appear and I did both tasks.

About halfway through the communion I jostled the cup. Some of the wine spilled on my hand. It spilled on the web of flesh between the index finger and the thumb of my left hand. This small accident was the beginning of the end of the pain that I had been suffering.

& & &

I first met Marshall when he was nine or ten. I was a church camp counselor and Marshall was a camper. I was flush with the belief I had the world by the tail. I had been a part of the radicalism of the 1960s and early 1970s and my recent religious conversion seemed to have added the missing element of that radicalism. I was alive with the power of being loved.

Marshall was a profoundly disturbed child who stayed to himself most of the time. A dark cloud seemed to hover over him. His smile did not fit the rest of his countenance. Marshall rarely spoke and when he did he either muttered to himself or made strange, guttural sounds. He seemed to enjoy those sounds, but they frightened other campers. He spoke to others only when they first addressed him. The strangest thing was his eyes. They had a helter-skelter quality to them. Perhaps his oddness was genetic or of chemical origin. Marshall was a lost child and I befriended him. In the joy of my newfound faith I believed that love could change the world.

Marshall noticed my attention. He grew deeply attached to me and showed his affection in little boy ways. By the end of camp I had on my dresser a pile of flowers, drawings, fossils which one could find on the property, and an assortment of other treasures. Marshall had brought me every one. We had connected. I know that at least once in his life he felt love. I in turn became very attached to this strange, troubled child.

After two summers as a counselor I was off to seminary with many happy memories of my time in camp. Marshall was one of them. I saw Marshall and his family from time to time when I was in and out of the diocese, but never expected to spend any more significant time with him. I had entrusted him into God's loving care. After graduation from seminary, I served for a time as an assistant in larger churches then moved to the first congregation of my own. It was in the small community where Marshall's family lived.

Marshall's father had committed suicide. I was told his father had been missing for a couple of days when his mother sent Marshall to his office to look for him. His father, a dentist, had killed himself in his office. Marshall found him.

His mother and I were friends, but she was a Roman Catholic and did not come to our parish. She was, however, happy for Marshall to come to the Episcopal Church. Marshall had found in the small congregation a place where he was loved. Every Sunday as we began worship, there sat Marshall, often with one or both of his sisters. The congregation loved Marshall dearly. Because of the odd and eerie things he did, many in the town gave him a wide berth. My congregation, however, welcomed Marshall as a member of the family. I had hoped that our love would exorcise the demons that seemed to haunt him.

I was wrong.

One lazy, sultry, summer day, tragedy struck. Marshall had just returned from his annual trip to camp and seemed happy—or as happy as he ever was. I was to have been out of town that weekend, but my plans had changed and Marshall didn't know that. I was about the only person with whom he ever discussed things that bothered him, and that was rarely. Our conversations were usually silent conversations.

Something was bothering Marshall, for that afternoon he shot himself in the head with a pistol in his bedroom.

Marshall's mother also thought I was out of town so she called her own priest. He came and gave Marshall last rites.

News travels rapidly in small towns, particularly bad news. I was at dinner with friends when the call came. By the time I reached the house they had taken Marshall's body away and arrangements for his funeral at the local Roman Catholic parish had been made. I was numb and sick. I did not feel guilt because he could not find me that day; I did feel a profound sadness that, though it has lessened over time, still abides.

Since the church things had been taken care of, I decided to do the only thing that remained to be done. With a couple who were close friends of Marshall's family I decided to clean up the bedroom where he had killed himself.

Three days later Marshall was buried.

This is where my memory of the event crystallizes and yet also grows foggy. I have thought and prayed about this a great deal over the years. I have pondered the nature of memory itself, especially remembrances of such awful events. Do we, over time, weave events into personal legend and mythology that then define us as persons? I know this is true of me with this story. I know my memories are "real," but the exact chronologies and connections are no longer clear. They have been filtered through both the despair I experienced following Marshall's death and the redemptive events that followed. The chronology is gone. But the visceral, bodily memories are vivid and detailed.

George, Patty, and I decided that cleaning up Marshall's bedroom was a trauma from which we could deliver his mother. I had experienced violence more than once in my life. I had witnessed it. I had received it. I had perpetrated it. But nothing could prepare me for what lay ahead.

Marshall's room reflected the disarray of his life. Papers, records, and other debris filled the floor. It was like entering a half-filled dumpster. I remember my anger at finding the inhalants that Marshall had been using. I also remember my horror at finding the only cover for the many 45 rpm records that were in the rubbish on the floor. The title of the song was "I'd Rather Be Dead."

The sense of clutter was the lesser of the two presences there. You could feel death and violence palpably. You could smell it. You could taste it. It was hideous. The blood and other human tissue was not the most frightening specter. The bullet hole in the wall was more horrifying. Though no bigger than my index finger, it loomed enormously and leered at us. My eyes unwillingly returned to it again and again.

We hurried to finish our task. None of us wanted to tarry. I do not remember a lot of conversation. I do remember a profound sense of communion among the three of us. George and Patty were very devout Catholics and had previously seen me as a "thief," stealing Marshall's soul from their church. After this shared experience, however, we became fast friends. This communion in the valley of death was the first of the graces that returned my hope, but I could not yet see the grace. I do not think that George, Patty, and I discussed what we had done for some time. Finally, George and I did talk, but it took copious amounts of alcohol to open us up. To this day we three are friends, friends bound by a baptism of blood.

Our task was done. I gathered the sheets and mattress and put them into the trunk of my car to take them to the dump. The drive was desolate enough, but the dump was worse. I remember thinking, "Is this it? Is this all that my friend means? Is this all that can be said for any of us? Is love not enough to change the world?" The scene at the dump was something out of a Kafka story. I remember a bull-dozer pushing the refuse of human lives into huge ditches in the ground. I remember the smoke from burning rubbish. I remember the cats picking the bones of what had been discarded by human beings. I did not want to consign my bloody treasures to this squalor. They were all that was left me of Marshall and I had paid a price to win them. After stalling as long as I could, I paid for the service and dumped my cargo.

As I drove home I noticed something. I had been careful not to get blood or other body debris on me. It was almost as if they were a contagion of violence and death. But as I drove I looked at my hands that had performed my last act of love and respect to my friend. On my left hand, in the web of flesh between my index finger and thumb, was Marshall's blood. It was not a lot of blood, but it covered a large area. I felt like Lady Macbeth. That "damned spot!" Yet it was also a treasure as my last possession of my friend. When I arrived home I washed my hands with mixed emotions. As with Lady Macbeth, the damned spot, though no longer there, remained. It does to this day. I see it from time to time. It still brings me sadness, but not as it did then. It also brings me solace.

In the daze that followed Marshall's death, I slipped into despair. I no longer had the world by the tail. I recall standing in my office envisioning a mental picture of all my hopes and dreams drifting away like sand. It was a desolating picture. All the fiery radicalism of my adolescence was gone. All the hope and joy of my conversion during the campus Jesus Movement had evaporated. All the complex theology I had acquired seemed gibberish. I considered quitting the priesthood. I could not see the grace already present in the midst of my desolation and the grace which would come. But come it did.

I am not sure how long it was between Marshall's death and my accident at the Sunday eucharist. I do not even remember to whom I was administering the cup. But I do remember the electricity when I looked down and saw Jesus' blood covering the same area of my hand as Marshall's had. It covered the whole of that damned spot, and no more. I stood and stared at it for what seemed hours, then wiped it off so that I could finish the task at hand. But it remained on my hand like the first damned spot. I wear it still. It is a sign of the paradox of God's love and goodness in the midst of awful events. Both spots are treasures now.

Is all this just accident and superstition? Perhaps, but I think not. This "accident" was the beginning of my healing. Grace in my new friendship with Patty and George had already manifested itself to me. From this point on it became more and more obvious. I began to see light and hope again. The desolation has never completely gone away. I still miss my strange, tormented friend. What made matters worse was that in the ensuing years I would bury three more children in fairly rapid succession. The last I loved as much as Marshall. But I was changed by the blood.

Psalm 31 contains the line, "Blessed be the Lord! For he has shown me the wonders of his love in a besieged city." I never understood that passage until after Marshall's death. I still have all the "why" questions about his death. I will never forget its horror. I have, however, regained my hope and belief that love does change the world. I no longer bear this belief with the simple flush of youth. It is more complex and profound. I no longer have any illusion about suffering and tragedy. But I now know of God's love in a besieged city.

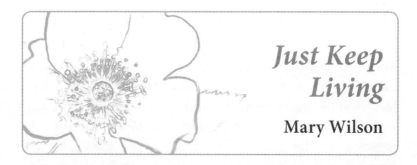

Just Keep Living

Mary Wilson

MARY WILSON was diagnosed with amyotrophic lateral sclerosis (ALS, or Lou Gehrig's disease) in 2004, at the age of forty-six. Living with ALS has taught her to distinguish what really matters from what does not, to see value and beauty in places she once overlooked, and to cope with adversity. When Forward Movement interviewed Mary in her home in 2006, the disease had progressed to a point where she was unable to speak clearly. She responded to questions by typing her answers onto a keyboard.

& & &

FM: *Tell us something about yourself and your background.*

Mary: I was born in 1957 in Cincinnati, Ohio, the fourth of six children in a Roman Catholic family. I graduated from high school and worked in the trust department of a bank. In 1981 I got married. Ron and I have a good marriage. We have a son and a daughter. Our daughter had her first child, a son, in May. I am now a grandmother! After our children were grown, I worked in the loan department of a bank for seven years until I had to retire because of my ALS in 2005. I have never had any other goals in life but a loving marriage, family, and friends.

FM: *Say something about the nature of ALS and how it affects you, physically, emotionally, and spiritually.*

Mary: ALS causes muscular deterioration which eventually paralyzes the body's muscles, including hands, arms, legs, feet, swallowing, speech, and breathing. The motor neurons in the brain and brain stem stop sending messages to the muscles, so the muscles eventually waste away and die. Researchers don't know why. There is no cure. Death is usually from suffocation when the lungs can no longer function. Life expectancy is usually two to five years after diagnosis, although 10 percent of people with ALS live as long as ten years with the disease. Heredity seems to be a factor in only 10 percent of cases. My mother died of ALS in 1991 when she was sixty-one and had had the disease for thirteen years. I was diagnosed in 2004 when I went to a doctor because my speech had become slurred and swallowing had become difficult. Now, two years later, my legs and right hand are weak—and Ron is the only person who can understand me when I speak!

FM: *What are some of the things you have had to learn, and how have you felt as these changes were occurring?*

Mary: I've learned to use a leg brace to keep my ankle from flopping, an automatic toothbrush, a food processor, a blender. To communicate, I use a hand-held personal digital assistant (PDA). I have a fax machine, email, and a free "text-to-speech" program on my computer. I'm lucky to have all that. My mother didn't have it. When strangers hear me talk, they sometimes think I've had too much to drink or am deaf. My mother dealt with that, too—people thought she was an alcoholic and talked to her loudly and slowly. I know what to expect; you get used to it. Losing the use of my legs was hard, but I get around with a walker, or in the future, with the power wheelchair my doctor ordered. Each limitation brings a new challenge. I felt that getting a walker was giving in to the disease, but I came to realize that it would help me continue to move around and not give up.

FM: *What has ALS taught you that you probably wouldn't have learned or discovered had you not gotten ALS?*

Mary: I've become more patient and more communicative. My illness doesn't just affect me; it affects everyone around me. I appreciate things more than I did before—family, friends, and nature. I've learned to accept that I can't do what I used to do. I'm grateful that I had the chance for fond memories of things like bowling, singing, and dancing.

We are taking more vacations, like a family camping trip to a local park for a week next month. This summer we will take an eleven-day Alaskan cruise and tour. I've discovered how caring people are, how willing they are to help. I get greeting cards from friends and my church telling me they are praying for me.

FM: *What was your initial reaction to the diagnosis of ALS? How have you moved forward from this initial reaction?*

Mary: I didn't feel well for a couple of years before I was diagnosed. I had a feeling something was wrong and that I was declining. When the doctor told me I had ALS, I wasn't surprised. In a way, I was relieved finally to know what was wrong. I had already dealt with the shock.

FM: *Describe how you felt toward God upon learning that you had ALS. How has this changed your faith?*

Mary: I don't blame God for being sick. I feel dying is as much a part of life as living. When people tell me they are praying for me, I ask them to pray for emotional strength and courage. I "talk" to God everyday. I enjoy watching a Catholic cable TV channel. Some people are praying for a miracle. I believe God works in ways we can't explain or understand. I believe miracles can come in many forms, sometimes in little things. My feelings toward God are stronger now. I'm home alone during the day, but don't feel alone because I believe God is with me. I ask God to help with little difficulties due to weakness, and thank him for the help and for just being with me. I'm learning more about the Catholic faith and the sacrament of healing of the sick, last rites, burial practices. I've also looked into other faiths' practices and beliefs. God travels down many avenues.

FM: *In light of your ALS, what has been most helpful in keeping you moving forward and staying positive about life?*

Mary: I try to live day to day, not let my limitations get me down. Depression is a common side effect of ALS. I keep myself busy to avoid that. I go bowling. Recently I had to quit actually bowling myself, but I still go to the bowling alley to cheer my team. I'm also the secretary/treasurer of two bowling leagues. And I'm knitting an afghan for my daughter. I love to read and play on the computer. Having a loving and supportive husband is a great help. I enjoy watching birds flip leaves in the yard looking for food, the trees swaying in the wind as if waving to God, the changes of the seasons, nature itself.

FM: *What advice do you have for people facing a situation such as yours?*

Mary: Allow a grieving period, but move on. Not letting yourself grieve can lead to denial and depression, but if you continue to grieve, you miss out on a lot. Knowing about your illness and what to expect can help, and acceptance can bring great peace. From what I've gone through so far, I can only say, "Just keep living!" Don't give up easily. Keep in touch with family and friends. It's going to hurt and be scary, but we are never alone unless we make it that way. Enjoy the time that is left with the people you love. Stay positive and social. Accept help, but don't expect it. Be patient with people who don't understand. Take time for yourself. Rest when you're tired.

FM: *What advice would you give to friends and family of someone with ALS or some other life-threatening disease?*

Mary: Treat the individual as a person, not a disease. Allow her to talk about her feelings, and share yours. Don't lose your sense of humor. If you're the primary caregiver, take time for yourself, too. If you're all stressed, that won't help. Treat the person who is sick the same way you would treat anyone else. Talk, cry, laugh, enjoy life together. Offer help, but don't be offended if it's not accepted. Share information about the disease and walk through it together. It helps to clarify things and talk them out. I was told by someone close that they heard my foot is numb, doesn't feel pain. That's not true. My foot doesn't bend like it did before ALS, but at this point of the disease, my foot is not numb. If I step on a rock, it will hurt. As the muscle damage progresses it may become numb when my foot is totally paralyzed. Be informed about what is happening.

FM: *What have family, friends, and others done that has helped you?*

Mary: It has been hard on my family. My experience reminds them of what my mother went through. It's all new to my friends; they didn't know anyone with ALS. What is helpful is staying in the social scene. I go with friends to professional football games, bowling alleys, parties, or just to their homes to watch television together. My brother, his wife, my husband, and I go and play cards once a month with my aunt, who is living in an assisted living facility. Strangers see me walking and ask if they can help, or try to catch me if they think I am falling. You hear about bad people all the time, but there are more good than bad people. I'm always surprised and grateful for their help.

FM: *What things became more important in your life and what things became less important as a result of your diagnosis?*

Mary: Just trying to keep going became more important. And of course learning about the facts and latest medical research about ALS. Then there are things like getting my finances in order and end-of-life issues. Family and friends become so much more important. And finishing a project, like the afghan I'm knitting while I still have use of my hands. When I could still use my legs, I organized closets so I could get to things as ALS progressed. Those may seem like little things, but they take on a new importance when you have a disease like ALS, and they give you a goal to work toward. Some things become less important, like purchasing anything for me that isn't useful, dwelling on the future (except in a practical way), having a perfectly clean house all the time, and petty arguments. Things I once might have argued about are just not important anymore.

FM: *Where do you see God in all this? Or, perhaps you don't see God in it?*

Mary: God is with everyone all the time. My belief in God hasn't changed because I am sick. I don't believe God makes people sick. It's just part of being human. I didn't ask God "Why me?" Why not me? There are people who live with physical limitations for decades. People fight illness and cope with tragedy every day. That my family and I are dealing with this just makes us part of a very, very large group of people. Everybody will die. I'm no different from anybody else. And I definitely see God in this! In every professional caretaker. In every stranger who offers help. In everyone who offers prayers. In the answers to problems that seem to come out of nowhere. In my prayers for peace and courage.

FM: *Any parting thoughts?*

Mary: Is there a heaven? I would like to think so! I would like to be in the presence of God and be reunited with loved ones who have moved on. But that is not for me to decide. What I can do is continue to honor God and treat everyone, including myself, lovingly.

SECTION II
Reflections

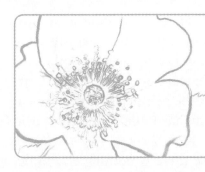

Losing
But Not Lost

Carol McCrea

Loss AFFECTS us in ways most of us would find unimaginable. It is apparent even at the cellular level. Every cell in our body, every organ, grieves. If it's too horrible, we try to run away from it, because deep down we know that if we stand and face it, we will be lured into jumping off a cliff or throwing ourselves onto the funeral pyre.

Some of us stare at the heart of the tragedy and cannot be pulled away from it as we watch in horror. We cannot eat, cannot sleep; our bodies throb with our longing for what is lost.

Deadly envy sets in toward all who still have theirs. We hate them. Their continuity, health, growth, and ongoing luck continuously remind us of what we do not have. We feel separated from fellow humans; there seems to be a glass wall between them and us. They have theirs; we do not have ours. How dare they go on as if nothing has happened? How dare they tell me about theirs? How cruelly they publicly celebrate their good fortune.

Rage erupts. Where shall we put it? On those who still have theirs? On those who *look* happy for whatever reason? On political leaders? On those who are privileged? Like the mothers who asked Solomon to judge whose baby it was, the mother whose baby had died did not care that another mother's baby would be split down the middle. It seemed fair. They would both get to suffer. It's better than suffering alone. Suffering easily crushes our compassion for others.

We thrash about for someone to blame—God, ourselves, the wealthy, the greedy, the new person, the different one, or the stranger. Somebody has to be blamed and held responsible.

Some of us go on because there is nothing else to do. Some of us will not go on, because to do so would demean our loss, so we dedicate the rest of our lives to that loss. Some of us hope there may be something better ahead, something to do, something to find, so we move ahead to find it.

Whom can we stand to be with? Perhaps only with other survivors of a similar tragedy. Who is left for us when we are bereft—child, spouse, lover, friends dead? Who can console us? Not those who have never had that experience. We can only be soothed by those who have had the same experience. We feel close to those who have similar losses and only to them. Eagerly we seek them out, or fearfully refuse to hear them because they remind us of our own pain. And do not talk of God to us. A god that permits such tragedy must be deaf to the pain of living beings. A god that wants us to suffer such tragedy in recompense for our sins is an unjust judge. A god that allows such horror has to be a monster.

Some of us may feel God does not love us or is punishing us. We wonder why we are singled out for this tragedy when others escape, survive, and even flourish.

And if there are too many losses, piled one on the other, what then? How can we bear it? How do we escape from the anger, the envy, the desire for revenge, the feeling of being squeezed under God's thumb? We cannot pretend it is not so. Pretense is madness. We cannot leap over these thoughts and feelings; they are part of the tragedy, perhaps the worst part as we relive it and chew it obsessively and taste the bitterness on our tongues.

We can freeze in this position, wither our growth, and be stunted for the rest of our lives. Or we can grow through the pain. It is our choice and ours alone. We get to decide. To wither is to die; to grow is to move in a different way, with a knot of pain at our core. But there comes a time when we have to resolve the issue for ourselves. We have to arrive at an explanation. We are driven to go deeper and not just stay at the level of loss and emotional pain. Buddhists detach and desire nothing. That is one way of moving out and away from the suffering. Saints transcend it, using altruism and compassion to rise above the horror and hopelessness to give meaning to their suffering. Christians have an additional agent to dig them out—the suffering, dying, and resurrected Jesus Christ.

In his life he experienced most, if not all, of the tragedies that humans can face. His family thought he was insane. His neighborhood rejected him. He was so weakened psychologically and spiritually that he could not perform miracles in his own town. Leaders of his religion conspired to kill him. He saw his friends and trusted companions disappear and disown him. He saw his career and work defiled. He saw his purpose misunderstood as revolt. The crowds that praised him and strewed branches and flowers in front of him turned against him and chose a murdering revolutionary instead of him to be freed from prison. He experienced the utter injustice of that. He experienced his close friend betraying him with a kiss—for money. His mother watched him die; he couldn't protect even her from the horror. It is not recorded that he knew the comfort of having a wife, lover, or child to bear his name.

In Gethsemane, he suffered wrenching anticipatory anxiety, knowing he was going to die, not a good, peaceful death, but a bad, torturous one. He was physically and mentally tormented and beaten; his skin flayed by whips and pointed thorns stuck into his head. Incarcerated with criminals, he was stripped and humiliated. He died slowly, achingly, mocked and slandered as he died. No comfort whatsoever. None. Not even contact with his Father.

Why? For us. So that we know forever that he endured whatever we have to endure. His dying encapsulates the love of God for us. He *gets* it. How could we have known that he *gets* it in any other way?

Only a dying, suffering Jesus, only a God willing to look on the painful loss of his Son, a God willing to lose, to feel, to experience human loss can do that. Only a vulnerable God can reach us in our own horror. If we have had gruesome physical or emotional pain, could we tolerate a God who had never experienced it? Never. If we have been outcast, rejected, abused, hated, stripped of love, compassion, and human dignity, only a God who had *been* there could minister to us. Anyone less would be the ultimate insult.

So we cry out to him in our anger, horror, and pain. He has been there himself and understands. He can and will lead us out. We have to do it, though, by crying out to him. We crave the unloading, the venting, and the peace that can happen when we do—as many times as we need to. Whatever the loss, horror, or tragedy, we have to be honest with ourselves and with our God.

Honesty is the means of healing. We are tempted to shout to God in anger, shake our fist, rage and rail at the heavens, and howl. And if we feel this way, we need to do it. We can yell at God the way a hurt child yells at a beloved parent. We can ask why. Where were you? Why did you let this happen?

"You could have stopped it," Mary said to Jesus, mourning her dead brother, Lazarus. Why didn't you stop it? Why me? Don't you care?

We see this happen in the story of Job. We see Job's answer: I am not God.

We cannot and never will understand. Our mortal brains are too small and too limited. They cannot encompass things vastly bigger than we are, the way ants on a leaf don't know that we have picked up the leaf in our hands and are moving them. An ant brain doesn't recognize that we are persons; to the ant we are just a large thing to climb.

We see this also happen in the story of the angel stopping Abraham from sacrificing his son in the ancient Canaanite practice, not unlike many sacrificial practices of ancient religions. God revealed himself to humans in human form, so we could understand him and his purposes.

In the death of his Son, Jesus Christ, God visually and historically showed us that he knows what we go through, and is on our side. In his death and resurrection, Jesus answers the question in a deeper way. His mission and reason for being, among others, is to be the link between God and humanity. Both human and divine, Jesus is the communicator between God and humans; he is the *logos*, the *Word*. And for those who do not understand words, he is the picture, the visual depiction of God's love as he suffers for us.

We need this love desperately, because in this life we are born to lose. In the best of circumstances—let's say, for example, a long, happy, and privileged life—we still will lose our work, our loves, our sight, hearing, health, friends, relatives, colleagues, lovers, spouses, bodies, and minds. What of those who never had these at all, or who lost them early?

We are destined to lose all. But we are not destined to be lost. We need to accept the fact of it, be gentle with ourselves and others on the way, and turn our faces like sunflowers to Jesus, who has gone the way before us and awaits us at the end.

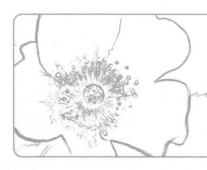

Praying for
Our Enemies

Francis H. Wade

ON SEPTEMBER 11, 2001, when our nation realized its vulnerability to evil, I was serving as rector of St. Alban's Parish in the target city of Washington, D.C. Our church is just a few yards from the Washington National Cathedral. In the confusion of that day, with smoke from the burning Pentagon smearing our southern horizon, the cathedral was considered a likely objective for a possible "next wave" of attacks. City and federal officials asked citizens to remain indoors. The cathedral was instructed to turn off the exterior lights that make it a beacon of peace in ordinary times but were spotlighting a target during this time of danger. It seemed to us at St. Alban's that the need for people to gather for prayer that night took precedence over the suggested curfew. With our great neighbor rendered mute by under-standable caution, we opened our doors for a service at 7 p.m. Word of mouth brought hundreds together for an extraordinarily powerful experience of raw emotion and spirit.

Preparing for the service was of necessity quick and, to our surprise, mainly easy. We had only to bring people to a point where they were aware of being in God's presence and then get out of the way, letting the Holy Spirit do the work of cleansing, healing, and focusing. At a time of great loss, fear, anger, and hope, words are not the most important things and sometimes just get in the way. There was, however, one point where words seemed to be wanted and were not provided by the traditional resources at hand. Jesus makes it abundantly clear that we are to pray for our enemies. But how, when those enemies had shattered not only so many real lives but also so many of our cherished illusions about our world and maybe even our God? We were not ready to begin sorting out what we needed to fight against, repent of, or mourn for.

These things are important and like most important things, they take time. I thought we needed to start praying for our enemies that night while the wounds were still fresh but I did not know what the prayer should be. It was easy enough to ask God to punish them, but that seemed more like praying *against* than *for* them. What do you say to God when you don't know what to say?

In Romans 8 we are told that the Holy Spirit will guide us when we do not know how to pray. I went to my computer as if it were a prayer desk with the fervent hope that something would emerge. This prayer almost leapt to the screen. It was completed in less than three minutes and in a way that allows me to take no credit for its composition.

A Prayer for Those Who Do Great Harm

Almighty God, whose will it is to place awe-some power into the hearts, minds, and hands of your children, let your care and our compassion be on those who do harm as well as those who are harmed. Lord, you reached across the limits of human understanding to embrace the outcast and the lost; reach now beyond our understanding and embrace those who have caused so much pain and death this day. We cannot but commend them to you, for in our hearts are seeds of hatred and in our nostrils the stench of madness. As you touch them in your healing ways, Lord God, dry also the hate that could grow in us, smother the fear that would blind us, and deliver us from the temptation to follow instincts that are far from the path you have set before us. In the Name of the One we always hope to follow, Jesus Christ, our Lord. *Amen.*

Over the years and in other times of pain and confusion, I have had reason to think about what this prayer assumes as well as what it says. Its first assumption is that human freedom is an awesome and, at the same time, an awful gift. In the Creation story we are told that people are made in the image of God. Many believe this refers to the capacity for choice that is bestowed so uniquely on human beings. The rest of creation lives with no choices or with choices severely circumscribed by instinct. As far as we know, we are the only ones with freedom to be what we were created to be—or to be far less.

The Genesis story of the Fall tells of the tragic consequences of choosing to be less. Adam and Eve lead the sad procession out of the Garden of God's Intent, but in their train follow multitudes of drunk drivers, abusers, self-centered manipulators, thoughtless injurers, and even fanatical murderers under the guise of "suicide" bombers. Despite all the pain our freedom has caused, God has so far not seen fit to remove it—perhaps because it is what makes us human, with all the gore and glory that implies. It is important to know that in or out of Eden we are never out of God's embrace. Human tragedy is a measure of our freedom and sin but it does not, never has, and never will limit God.

As St. Paul says "Neither death, nor life, nor angels, nor rulers, nor things present, nor things to come, nor powers, nor height, nor depth, nor anything else in all creation, will be able to separate us from the love of God in Christ Jesus our Lord" (Romans 8:38-39).

The prayer asks God to help us direct compassion toward our enemies. This is a hard task, for compassion in these times is almost impossible to find much less direct toward those who hurt us. Suffering is by its very nature self-centered. Whether we stub our toe in the dark or are ambushed by evil, pain makes it hard to consider others' needs, especially when that "other" is the cause of our pain. It is not easy, but if it were easy we would not have to ask God to help us do it. And it is vital that we make that turn from inward pain to outward compassion. Anne Morrow Lindbergh, who was no stranger to suffering, once wrote:

> I do not believe that sheer suffering teaches.
> If suffering alone taught, all the world would
> be wise, since everyone suffers. To suffering
> must be added mourning, understanding,
> patience, love, openness and the willingness
> to remain vulnerable.*

Such a journey to wholeness must be done with God's help for none of us is capable of it on our own.

Finally the prayer recognizes the great danger this kind of pain sets in our path. Hatred that is easy to justify is difficult to shed. Hatred retained can metastasize and consume as vigorously as any cancer. The fear of vulnerability that pain establishes in us can paralyze our ability to love and

---

* Anne Morrow Lindbergh, *Hour of Gold, Hour of Lead—Diaries of Anne Morrow Lindbergh 1929-1932* (New York: Harcourt, Brace, Jovanovich, 1973), p. 214.

even our ability to live. And anger at the manner in which our enemies have behaved can seduce us into becoming their disciples instead of our Lord's. For what is a disciple but one whose actions imitate those of his master? If our behavior resembles that of our enemies more than that of our Lord, whose disciples are we? Hatred, fear, and temptation are a slippery slope on which we need to hold tightly to the Lord's outstretched hand. It is hard. That is why we pray.

& & &

What do we do when our instinct or experience tells us that God is the enemy? Where do we turn when our pain is rooted in what appears to be an exercise of God's power to destroy (earthquake, fire, or flood) or a withholding of God's power to save (illness, accident, or birth defect)? We can readily see the advantage of asking God's help in responding to human enemies. Where do we turn when we are angry with God?

The answer is not always clear, but the steps to take are clear. In a healthy relationship (and let us assume that God's perfect love shown in Jesus Christ does establish such a relationship) three things are always possible. One is anger. Shallow relationships are too fragile to bear it, but deep ones are strong and resilient. Loving relationships always have room for anger, disappointment, and frustration. It really is okay to be angry with God—take a look at the prophet Jeremiah, or Jonah, or the Psalms.

The second is confrontation. It is rarely possible to speak candidly with our human enemies, but it is always possible with God. When we are angry with God we can say so. God does not thereby become accountable to our anger or offer detailed explanations of why life unfolds as it does. What I usually find is a reminder that God's ways are not my ways (Isaiah 55:8-9), and that God "does not willingly afflict or grieve" us (Lamentations 3:33 and *The Book of Common Prayer,* Prayer #55, page 831).

While this is not the rationale, defense, or apology we really want, it is enough to allow us to move to the third step, which is forgiveness. We might be uncomfortable with the notion of forgiving God, but as with anger, healthy relationships have a capacity for forgiveness. Our absolution in this case is simply an affirmation that the future is more important than the past. Life moves only in one direction, and that is forward into the future. The past may or may not be crowned with understanding, justification, or pleasure, but life is found only in front of us. Forgiveness is the means by which we let go of a piece of the past in order to take up the future. Maintaining the healthy relationship with God is vital if we expect that future to avoid the devastating effects of hatred, fear, and anger cited above.

Dear friend, if you have read this far, I assume the pain of loss has come into your life or into the life of someone near you. I am sorry that this is your moment to share the universal experience of suffering. I wish I could explain it away or make it easy, but I cannot. I can, however, tell you that the effects of this kind of distress are well known. Pain powerfully pulls us into ourselves, curling us into mental and emotional fetal positions where we can become locked and paralyzed, cut off from the life that continues to unfold before us. For that reason, when you can, and as soon as you can, I beg that you begin the reopening that is a return to life. An early step in that return is to pray for our enemy whether that enemy is a child of God or God himself.

Why Does God Not Stop It?

Desmond Tutu

WHENEVER a disaster such as the tsunami in 2004 or Hurricane Katrina in 2005 devastates our land, or a more personal disaster such as the death of a loved one after a painful illness occurs, then in our distress and bewilderment most of us cry out in our anguish, "Where is God? Why does God not stop this?"

The first thing to do is always to convey our deep sympathies to those who have been afflicted.

Some of the attempts to explain God's ways are less than helpful, and can themselves add to the anguish of the afflicted. They are often too glib and exacerbate the dereliction and pain of those afflicted. The purveyors of such explanations are sometimes dubbed Job's comforters, for being too clever by half, as were those who tried to comfort Job. When he suffered so grievously, they spewed forth the orthodoxy of the day with its retributive view of all suffering, that it was dire punishment for the victim's wrongdoing. You want to ask what wrong a baby who dies of leukemia is thought to have committed to deserve such an early death. Such explanations are less than helpful; they depict a God few of us would want to worship. So I urge that we have a degree of agnosticism, for we cannot hope to know everything there is to know. Ultimately it is a mystery which we want to do our best to understand.

The Dilemma

Theological students quite early in their studies encounter the so-called "problem of evil." It is a problem that is usually posed as a dilemma. Either God is good and wishes only good for us, but is not omnipotent and so cannot stop the evil and suffering; or God is omnipotent, but not good, and so will not stop it. This will not do. It is a problem for us because we believe that God is both all good and all powerful. That is precisely why we are so agitated.

Suggested Solution

One of the exhilarating things we believe is that this omnipotent God, who can do anything consistent with his goodness, for our sakes places constraints on his power. God has given us a real, albeit creaturely and limited, autonomy. God has endowed us with free will and holds our free will in reverence, respects our freedom, our creaturely autonomy, and will usually do nothing to undermine or violate it. God allows us to choose either to love or to hate, to obey or to disobey. That is important when we discuss the problem of suffering because much human suffering is due to wrong choices that we make. The Holocaust happened because certain people decided that Jews, gypsies, and homosexuals had to be eliminated. Our God is breathtaking in the respect he has for our freedom. To have stopped the Holocaust would have required God to intervene to stop those who were making those decisions from making them. Then what price our freedom to be moral, decision-making persons?

Or look at the case of Hurricane Katrina. It was a human decision to build New Orleans below sea level with all the hazards that entailed. Even more seriously, it has been alleged that the levees failed because adequate funding to build effective levees was reduced and diverted to other items such as the Iraq war. To reverse those decisions, God would have had to deny American politicians their freedom and turn them into automatons. They would no longer have been persons. They would have been incapable of wrong decisions because their freedom had been undermined and violated. God wants our love and God wants it to be freely given, not coerced.

That is the price we must pay to be moral beings.

We inhabit a universe with laws that are consistent, predictable, and reliable. Otherwise, it would not be an ordered universe but chaos. Suppose we saw a baby falling out of a fourth floor window. It would be wonderful if somehow the ground where she was going to land turned soggy so she would land gently. But what would then happen to the car that was driving past that spot when it suddenly encountered not a hard surface but a soft and soggy one? Or if the law of gravity were suspended for a moment so that the dear baby did not plummet to the ground but floated in midair? That would be wonderful for her, but what would happen to the buildings in the vicinity without gravity? They might start floating about themselves, and imagine the chaos that would result! We inhabit a universe of natural laws of cause and effect. It is a stable, reliable environment in which it is possible to plan and to live an orderly life. But it imposes limitations and restrictions.

It is also suggested that Hurricane Katrina was so devastating because of global warming caused by our wanton pollution of the atmosphere with destructive gases being emitted and the ozone layer being depleted by the folly of human action. God could stop this only by nullifying our freedom to choose.

God has taken a huge gamble that we will want to be his collaborators to help him make an imperfect world slightly better. We have been thrilled by the extraordinary outpouring of compassion and sympathy for those who have to bear the brunt of these and other disasters.

The rabbis say God created an imperfect world so that we would partner with him to make it a better home for us all. Compassion and gentleness and courage would be meaningless in a world that did not have the needs that characterize our world. Courage is devoid of any significance when there is nothing to fear. This is also true of attributes such as patience.

Our God is omnipotent but is also impotent. God does not compel us to be good, to make the right choices. No, God can only woo us, offering us the gift of grace so that we will make the right decisions. But we must appropriate, accept, and use the gift. God does not ram it down our throats. God waits for us to make the right decision. It is a glorious picture of how deeply God respects us.

And God, in our faith, does get involved in our anguish and suffering. God is Immanuel, God with us, who, as in the story of the three faithful servants, enters the fiery furnace into which his servants have been thrown. God does not give good advice from a safe distance. In Jesus Christ, God enters our human condition to redeem it.

They tell the story of a young Jew in a concentration camp, a mere boy. There was one Nazi guard who tried to make his life even more miserable. He insulted and tormented him heartlessly. One day the Jew was ordered to clean out the latrines. As he stood in the filth his tormentor stood above him and mocked him asking, "Where is your God now?" The Jewish boy replied quietly, "He is right here with me in this muck."

Our God is right there with us in all our anguish and grief and bewilderment. He loves us with a love that will not let us go, a love that is unchanging and unchangeable. We are each precious to him. Our names are engraved on God's hands. He knows each of us by name, for the very hairs of our head are numbered. And he wants to wipe the tears away from our eyes, for ultimately,

> *Neither death nor life,*
> *Nor angels nor principalities...*
> *Nor heights nor depths,*
> *Nor anything in all creation*
> *Can separate us from the love of God*
> *in Christ Jesus.*
>
> —Romans 8:38-39

Whether you are a Christian or not, God loves you with a love that will not let you go. Whether you are a Christian or not, you are precious to God with a preciousness that cannot be computed. God is there with you in the awfulness and darkness of your anguish and suffering. God will never desert you.

Against Explanation and for Consolation

John J. Thatamanil

READING the newspapers in the weeks after the December 2004 tsunami was for me nearly as heartbreaking and faith-shaking as reading the first accounts of the tragedy. The initial news was overwhelming. How, after all, does one begin to think about the death of 200,000 people, perhaps a third of whom were children? How does one register the force and reality of entire villages vanishing in raging waters?

But what has moved me again to grief, frustration, and even anger is what has transpired since then: the religious attempt to make sense of this tragedy. A wide variety of Christian and other religious thinkers have suggested that in the tsunami they have seen God's judgment and punishment at work.

Some of the words have been impious. To suggest that God would deprive thousands of mothers and fathers of their children to concentrate our minds on the death and resurrection of his Son gives us a god unworthy of worship, a god bearing no resemblance to the God proclaimed by that very Son.

The news from other religious traditions is no better. Among Buddhists and Hindus, the question is not one of God's responsibility but of human agency. Karma is the culprit. Those who suffered and died did so because of their actions in this life or lifetimes past.

Amy Waldman, in an article published in *The New York Times* on January 12, 2005, described the following scene in a small town in Sri Lanka:

> Next door to four houses flattened by the tsunami, three rooms of Poorima Jayaratne's home still stood intact. She had a ready explanation for that anomaly, and her entire family's survival: she was a Buddhist, and her neighbors were not.
>
> "Most of the people who lost relatives were Muslim," said Ms. Jayaratne, adding for good measure that two Christians were also missing. As proof, she pointed to the poster of Lord Buddha that still clung to the standing portion of her house.

After hearing this litany of judgment and self-righteousness from the religious, I find myself in sympathy with scientifically minded atheists and secularists. Knowledge of plate tectonics and an appreciation of wave dynamics is worth more than everything religious people offer by way of explanation. Scientific explanations are not immoral, as religious explanations often are. Scientists do not blame dead children for picking a bad day to play on the beach. Only the religious do that.

Given the inadequacy of religious attempts to explain suffering, should we abandon faith entirely and devote ourselves to such knowledge as we can gain from the sciences? If the central task of religion is explanation, then the answer is yes. We should free ourselves from these religious explanations. They become temptations either to complacency or judgment. They distance us from the pain of those who grieve by giving to such suffering an air of necessity, or inevitability. If the victimized, the poor, and the oppressed suffer because of their karma or because of God's judgment, then such suffering, far from being an offense, becomes a necessary part of the fabric of an orderly universe, something to be accepted, even applauded. To commit ourselves to such a vision is to compound tragedy with the unnecessary evil of an unfeeling heart.

But what if religion is not a matter of explanation but of consolation? Religions have sometimes sought to provide consolation by way of explanation. That effort has been ambiguous at best and criminal at worst. Consolation does not come by way of explanation.

The great earthquake of 1755 laid waste the entire city of Lisbon on All Saints' Day, while most of its residents were at worship. Voltaire commented in his *Philosophical Dictionary* that "the problem of good and evil remains an inexplicable chaos for those who seek in good faith. It is an intellectual exercise for those who argue: they are convicts who play with their chains."

Convicts who play with their chains! An apt description of theologians. The author of the Book of Job would have agreed with the French philosopher. Secularists and skeptics are not alone in condemning facile theologians and their attempts to explain away suffering.

The Book of Job begins with a prose prologue in which God and the *satan*—not the pointy horned figure we know and dread, but a figure who keeps company in God's heavenly courts, God's chief prosecutor—are having a conversation. God asks Satan to consider the exemplary virtue of his servant Job. But the prosecutor replies that Job's faithfulness is due entirely to the material blessings and protection God has given Job. The prologue establishes right up front that Job is innocent, faithful, and just.

The prologue also places before us several perplexing questions. Will Job continue to worship God when no material gain can come from such worship? Is commitment to God a transaction, like buying insurance? Is human faithfulness contingent on divine blessing? And what are we to say about a God who permits the innocent to suffer? Is God unjust? How do we speak of God when faced with the suffering of the innocent? The Book of Job raises these questions and forbids us from turning away.

What then of Job's friends, these theologians extraordinaire? How do they respond to their friend? What do they say about God in the face of Job's suffering? Initially his friends say absolutely nothing:

> Now when Job's three friends heard of all these troubles that had come upon him, each of them set out from his home....They met together to go and console and comfort him. When they saw him from a distance, they did not recognize him, and they raised their voices and wept aloud; they tore their robes and threw dust in the air upon their heads. They sat with him on the ground seven days and seven nights, and no one spoke a word to him, for they saw that his suffering was very great.
>
> —Job 2:11-13

Before we criticize Job's friends, we should ask whether our own ability to keep company with those caught up in desolation and sorrow is any better. Often we recoil and turn away. Job's friends do not turn away. To their credit, they sit in silent solidarity with the sufferer. This is our first obligation in the face of tragedy and grief: to keep silent solidarity with the suffering.

But there is also a time to speak. Every pastor or hospital chaplain knows that the cry of "Why?" comes unbidden and spontaneously to the lips of those who suffer, as it does for Job. What then are we to do, we who dare to speak in the name of God?

I cannot answer that question. But I believe that we can learn something about what to say and not say by watching Job's friends run aground.

In the depth of his agony, Job begins the conversation by wishing that he had never been born and cursing the very day of his birth:

> *Why did I not die at birth,*
> *come forth from the womb and expire?*
> *Why were there knees to receive me,*
> *or breasts for me to suck?*
> *For then I should have lain down and been quiet;*
> *I should have slept; then I should have been at rest.*
>
> —Job 3:11-12

How familiar and painful these words are to any who have kept company with the acutely injured, those who have lost dear ones, people caught up in depression, the suicidal, those who long for the rest of death rather than the torture of living. But Job's lament differs from those we often hear in one respect: Job maintains clarity of vision because he unwaveringly asserts his own innocence. He does not blame himself for his suffering. Yet his friends cannot countenance this because it disrupts their theological moorings.

For Job's friends, everything is clear: The world is an orderly place that runs according to a strict moral logic. God punishes the guilty and blesses the innocent. Job is suffering, which means God is punishing him. And since God never punishes the innocent, Job must be guilty, his protests not-withstanding. His friend Eliphaz begins, "Think now, who that was innocent ever perished? Or where were the upright cut off? As I have seen, those who plow iniquity and sow trouble reap the same. By the breath of God they perish, and by the blast of his anger they are consumed" (4:7-9).

His friend Bildad even has the temerity to pass judgment on the children Job has lost. "How long will you say these things, and the words of your mouth be a great wind? Does God pervert justice? Or does the Almighty pervert the right? If your children have sinned against him, he has delivered them into the power of their transgression" (8:1-4).

Don't protest too quickly against this theology—it has a good claim to being both biblical and logical. Eliphaz's words nicely echo Psalm 1:

> *Blessed is the man who walks not in the*
> *counsel of the wicked...*
> *his delight is in the law of the Lord...*
> *He is like a tree planted by streams of water,*
> *that yields its fruit in its season*
> *and its leaf does not whither...*
> *The wicked are not so,*
> *but are like chaff which the wind*
> *drives away.*
>
> —Psalm 1:1-4

People today also cite scripture and mount arguments that run roughshod over the suffering. Job's more fortunate friends do well to keep company with Job. But when Job speaks from his suffering and anguish, his words disturb his friends. Job had once subscribed to his friends' theology, but now he finds that theology breaking down. He can no longer believe that those who suffer do so because they deserve to suffer. That during his prosperous years Job had never allowed his theology to interfere with the work of doing justice and looking after the needs of the poor is to his credit. But now that he finds himself on the other side of the table, he can no longer accept a morally tidy universe in which the good prosper and the wicked perish. He knows better. And so do we.

Faced with clinging to an unworkable theology or entering into their friend's suffering, Job's friends stay with their theology.

෫ ෫ ෫

Let us not be too quick to judge. To give up our classroom theology is easy. It's something else to surrender the theology we live by. To give that up is to be broken open, to find that our way of living in the world doesn't work. To surrender our day-to-day living theology is to become vulnerable, raw, and naked to the suffering of others without the armor of mediating categories. It is not easily done. Given a choice between saving our comfortable and well-worn theologies and entering into vulnerable solidarity with those who suffer, we must always choose the latter.

You may ask, "How are we to know whether and when the theology that has sustained us needs to drop away?" Here too, Job enlightens us. As we listen to Job's laments, we are initially provoked by his pain and anguish. But as we follow his conversations with his friends, Job's private grief becomes a collective lament on behalf of all who suffer.

Personal anguish often encloses us in the prison of private pain. This is especially so for those whose suffering is mainly psychological. Not surprisingly, that is where Job begins. But then something happens. When Job gives up the idea that the unfortunate deserve their suffering, he departs from a world divided between the righteous/prosperous on one hand and the wicked/accursed on the other. Now he casts his lot with the suffering innocent. He can protest on their behalf:

> Why are not the times of judgment kept
> > by the Almighty,
> and why do those who know him never
> > see his days?
> The wicked remove landmarks;
> > they seize flocks and pasture them.
> They drive away the ass of the powerless;
> > they take the widow's ox for a pledge.
> They thrust the poor off the road...
> There are those who snatch the orphan child
> > from the breast,
> and take in pledge the infant of the poor...
> > —Job 24:1-4, 9

What do we learn from Job's transformation?

Nothing spoken about suffering is true if it sunders the beloved community. No word about suffering can be right if it divides people. We must discard any and every theology that disrupts our capacity to form community with "the least of these," our neighbors. We must cast away any theology that sanctions the status quo by declaring the privileged blessed and the poor accursed.

There is another lesson from Job's transformation. If forced to choose between defending God and defending the downtrodden, we must choose the latter. God does not need our defending. Those who suffer do. Any theology that invests more in defending God's innocence than in defending those who are the beloved of God misses the mark. We must not preserve God's reputation at the expense of the suffering.

Job eventually gives up on his conversation with his friends, whom he rightly calls "worthless physicians." Then, remarkably, Job turns from talking about God to talking with God. Direct address and prayer replace disputation.

It is a wonder that Job is not put off from speaking to God by the theological machinations of his friends. Those who attempt to explain run the risk of driving their listeners to despair. Let us pray that, like Job, our listeners turn from talking about God to talking with God.

When Job does address God, God responds. He vindicates Job, silences Job's friends, and then corrects Job as well. First, God repudiates the logic of his self-appointed defenders. God explicitly states that they have spoken wrongly about the divine nature. God refuses to accept the role of moral enforcer who always rewards the righteous and punishes the guilty. No such god can be a God of grace.

But God also dismisses Job's accusations that God has treated Job unjustly. Job is right to protest his innocence. God agrees. As Dominican priest and Peruvian theologian Gustavo Gutierrez has shown, Job still remains captive to the logic of innocence and guilt that he is learning to outgrow. If I suffer but know myself to be innocent, Job reasons, then it follows that I suffer wrongly. Therefore, God must be guilty (someone must be guilty), and if not me, then God. That logic leaves the dichotomy of innocence and guilt in place. To undercut it, God resorts to sarcasm. He gives Job a vision of the immense scale of the creation and God's creative power:

> *Where were you when I laid the foundation*
> *of the earth?*

Tell me, if you have understanding.
Who determined its measurements—surely
you know!...
Have you commanded the morning since
your days began,
and caused the dawn to know its place?...
Where is the way to the dwelling of light?
—Job 38:4, 5, 12, 19

On and on God's interrogation goes, forcing Job to acknowledge that God's universe is not made to the scale of Job's moral logic. Thanks to the sciences of our day, we too are growing to realize the unimaginable scale of the universe as we come to appreciate our fragile place in interstellar space.

Yet even as God presses upon Job a sense of his smallness relative to the vastness of God's creation, Job also comes to see that the God who can hook Leviathan like a fish is nonetheless speaking to him. To be addressed by God is simultaneously to recognize both our smallness in God's universe and the dignity of the self whom God addresses.

The Book of Job never says that Job is satisfied by what God has to say. God offers no explanation. What consoles Job is the experience of God in the midst of devastation: "I had heard of thee by the hearing of the ear, but now my eye sees thee" (42:5). God consoles only by way of presence. We should not try to do what God declines to do—we cannot explain. But we can console. We glorify God not by justifying God's ways and not by establishing who is or is not guilty. No amount of argumentation and explanation will glorify God. We glorify God when, by God's grace, we become agents of healing and consolation.

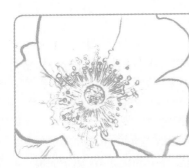

Passing Through the Door

Frederick W. Schmidt

TALLMANSVILLE, W. Va., Jan. 10 (AP) — For three wonderful hours, Sago Baptist Church was home to a miracle.

For almost two days, the families of 13 miners trapped deep underground in the mine just across the hollow believed that if they prayed hard enough, sang hymns loud enough, God would deliver their fathers, brothers, sons and friends safely through the doors of the little church founded 150 years ago.

When word arrived that 12 had survived, the tiny white clapboard church shook with spontaneous screams of joy and the near-hysterical laughter of intense relief.

All the glory was given to God, and to the pastor who had kept the flames of their faith stoked during the long, long wait.

That word was wrong...

The only miner to come through the doors of Sago Baptist, parishioner Fred Ware Jr., did so Monday in a casket...

"I can't understand why it happened like it did, but we don't question God," said church trustee John Casto. "God knows what he's doing."

—Vicki Smith, Associated Press, January 10, 2006

BRUTALLY, abruptly, suffering brings us to the edge of despair. There, at the precipice—at that point where love and life appear to have been extinguished—we reach for a miracle. But what does it mean when only the dead return to pass through our doors? To discover that the disease will not go away, that the handicap will forever shape our lives, that my child will not return, that the job cannot be recovered, that the relationship cannot be salvaged, or that my home cannot be repaired?

In the moments when the prayer for deliverance that we lifted to God goes unanswered we reach instinctively for explanations. God must have had another plan in mind—a deeper, inscrutable purpose. I must not have prayed hard enough, often enough, or ardently enough. God is trying to teach me something, bring me to a new place, or use me in a new way.

More often than not this inevitable, altogether human, and anguished search for an explanation for suffering proves fruitless. Deeper virtue may arise out of an experience of loss, but some are simply hardened and disillusioned by it. There are times when our suffering may arise from our sinfulness, but much of it does not. Good is often frustrated, bitterness persists where virtue flourished, the faithful are seemingly overwhelmed, and suffering is often marked by senseless loss.

The experience of Jesus in the Garden of Gethsemane acknowledges our longing for deliverance, but clearly as followers of Jesus we cannot live in dependence upon our prayers for it. Underlining the turmoil Jesus experienced as he faced the prospect of suffering and death, the Gospel of Mark clearly suggests that Jesus anticipated his betrayal, agonized over the failure of his disciples to remain awake and pray with him, and then finally watched them flee, leaving him to face torture and crucifixion alone (Mark 14:32-50).

Standing at the precipice where love and life appear to have been extinguished, Jesus prays, "Abba, Father, for you all things are possible; remove this cup from me; yet, not what I want, but what you want." Jesus asks for deliverance, but he is not delivered. He surrenders to God, not to the circumstances. His death felt to him as final as ours feels to us. The resurrection was neither anticipated nor scripted. It does not follow naturally from Jesus' death. Though reversed, death is never denied. Death is real.

Drawing on a long, rich biblical tradition that has always mistrusted the insistence that prayers for deliverance are the only ones that matter and the argument that good things happen to good people, Mark uses the experience of Jesus to challenge our dependence upon signs and wonders. But his gospel also offers us hope that arises from the experience of Jesus. Addressed directly to our own suffering, hear the words Jesus might speak to us:

> *My child, suffering is neither the measure of your goodness, nor of God's love for you.*

In seeking an explanation for the misfortunes we encounter, we often scrutinize our behavior, looking for choices that may have placed us in harm's way or displeased God, prompting him to withdraw his love. Having an explanation for suffering—even one that places the blame squarely on our own behavior—is often preferable to the seemingly senseless character of the suffering we experience; and there are times, of course, when our actions do bring suffering with them.

Mark would remind us, however, that this is not the whole truth. Jesus suffers, not because of his own choices, but because of the choices made by his contemporaries, abetted by the cowardice and treachery of his followers. The righteous do suffer and often without explanation. From passages elsewhere in his gospel, the evangelist would also remind us that on occasion we may place ourselves beyond the reach of God's love, or our life's circumstances may make it difficult for us to feel the love of God. But God never ceases to love us, nor actively withdraws his love from us.

> *My child, the prayer for deliverance—though often unanswered—is a natural part of prayer, the honest expression of our heart's deepest longing at a time of crisis.*

Prayer is among life's most intimate activities, an opening of our lives and hearts to God, marked by a knowledge of who we are in the deepest and fullest sense. In prayer lifted both with and without words, we lay bare our deepest longings, our greatest joys, and the true state of our soul. That our prayers may be marked by raw need and give expression to sharp pain that prompts us to cry out for deliverance is, therefore, no surprise. Prayer would not be prayer if it lacked the vulnerable honesty that accompanies such intimacy.

Mark is aware of this and describes the prayer of Jesus in Gethsemane as a moment filled with anguish. He describes his prayer without asking whether it is theologically appropriate and without reassuring us that Jesus prayed with faith. Honest, even ambivalent about the prospect of being delivered, Mark reminds us in describing the scene in Gethsemane that prayer is not something to be polished and sanitized, a performance marked by rock-solid certitude, but by a willingness to trust God with the state of our soul.

> *My child, as difficult as it may be from time to time, your life is lived out in the Kingdom's dawning.*

The light that accompanies the Kingdom's arrival breaks across the landscape of our lives, filling some places with the brightest of light while leaving other places in relative darkness. Scripture witnesses to the goodness of God and to the importance of prayer, but that witness is framed by a candid acknowledgement that there is much that remains incomplete as long as we live in this world.

Our lives are marked by shattered hopes, half-fulfilled dreams, and sin. This means we are not always delivered from danger. At the same time, however, we affirm that the Kingdom has begun to spread across our lives and that the time will come when we will live fully in its light.

> *My child, it may be hard to accept, but know that resurrection, not deliverance, is the pattern that finally defines my Father's work in our world.*

Human experience teaches us that frailty and mortality are givens and that, sooner or later, prayers for deliverance go unanswered. But we are not left alone. The promise is that God in Jesus Christ is Immanuel—God with us, all the way.

Entering into that experience at Gethsemane, Jesus faces a death no less real than our own. He faces that death without knowing how God will respond. Resurrection is not a sequel to his death or ours. It is a reversal, God's "no" to death's effort to dominate us.

> *My child, I did not call you to surrender to life's circumstances, but to the Father in the midst of life's circumstances.*

In surrendering at a time of loss, we make ourselves available to God's purposes. The good that flourishes in the midst of suffering flourishes in spite of it, not because of it. Suffering may radicalize life. It may convince us that we have majored on the minor and minored on the major. But it is only by trusting in God that the power of the resurrection is released in our lives.

When Jesus prays, "not what I want, but what you want," he is not giving voice to a brand of religious fatalism. He is giving expression to his confidence in God. Paul would later make a similar and important distinction. Writing to the church in Rome, he observed not that all things are good, but that "all things work together for good *for those who trust in God.*"

> *My child, the loss you have experienced is real,*
> *but you need not be overcome by it.*

The losses experienced at the precipice of life lack the power to drive us over the edge and out of God's reach. The body may return, passing lifeless through the doors of the church. But as we were in baptism and in life, the Christian is taken up in the larger reality that is the life of God in Christ. Our lives, our faith, and our hope do not rise or fall on prayers for deliverance that are answered. They depend upon the One who, like us has passed through the door to rise again.

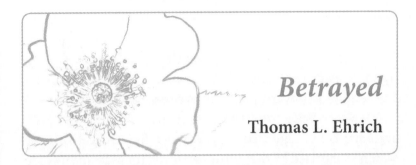

Betrayed

Thomas L. Ehrich

To DEAL with suffering, sometimes we need to deal with betrayal.

We know that suffering happens. We know that storms strike, wars break out, people get sick and die, workers lose their jobs, crops die in the field. Our journey through life will be bumpy.

Suffering still hurts, especially when it happens to seemingly innocent ones like children. But we know to expect tough times. We are frail, and people around us are frail. As M. Scott Peck said in the opening line of *The Road Less Traveled*, "Life is difficult."

We also know that not all suffering scenarios are the same. Some people seem to get more than their share: surviving one cancer and soon developing another, losing one job and then another. We know not to expect fairness in the parceling out of pain.

Then comes a Hurricane Katrina. The familiar warnings go out, weather channels track the storm, and we watch from afar as people decide whether to evacuate. Storm hits, levees break, streets flood. Worse than usual, tragic for those in Katrina's path, but localized, nothing that would shake our foundations.

Then comes the aftermath. Suddenly we realize that fundamental systems have crashed. Civility and law enforcement break down. Emergency shelters are quickly overwhelmed. Communications systems are no better than they were on September 11. At every level, from the President taking a fly-by to disaster relief specialists clueless about disaster relief, the systems of government fail. We see it all on television.

It gets worse from there. It turns out the levees were systematically neglected. It turns out key federal officials weren't surprised by the storm's severity; they just didn't care. The war in Iraq had depleted National Guard troops and equipment. The predominantly black face of New Orleans' agonies revealed longstanding systemic issues that Mardi Gras revelers hadn't seen. Now the wealthy are cashing in on reconstruction.

Now it sinks in: many basic systems don't work, much of the safety net is shredded, government responds poorly to other situations of need. Now the pieces fall in place. Larger scenarios come into focus. What we thought would see us through tough times—medical care, education, jobs, pensions, personal safety, government benefits—seems to be in disarray. Now we see the physician who is too busy avoiding lawsuits to provide effective care. Now we count the school hours devoted to meaningless testing. Now we notice stories about pension funds being raided by inept corporate managers. Now we realize that we are expendable to our employers. Now we sense the dangers of predators on the Internet, mercenary banks sending us credit cards we don't need.

Now we find ourselves in the land of Betrayal. The lens has turned, and what we took in stride before now seems to signal betrayal by forces that mean us ill. Trust is broken, confidence is lost, our sense of a greater good is gone. This is more than bad luck or an untimely storm. This is treachery, being deserted in time of need.

Thomas L. Ehrich   _Comfort Ye_

Not all suffering stems from betrayal. But more and more frequently, disasters like Katrina and the December 2004 tsunami reveal underlying disarray: failed systems, corrupt and incompetent officials, warnings ignored or not given, impacts falling hardest on the poor, squandered resources. The same is true with tragedies like the September 11 attacks, systemic issues like evaporating jobs and economic suffering, and avoidable illnesses associated with environmental degradation and the merchandising of poor diet. The cumulative impact is shattering.

Suffering in a trustworthy world is one thing. We learn to support each other and to count on better days. Suffering in the disarray of betrayal is quite another thing. It leaves us isolated, untrusting, defensive, more inclined to pull inside some safe place than to extend a hand outward. We blame, rather than resolve.

We don't normally approach suffering with the possibility of betrayal in mind. We approach suffering as a pastoral issue, perhaps counting on the five stages of grief to make sense of our emotions and responses. We approach suffering as a temporary crisis to be managed. We approach suffering as a personal crisis, perhaps involving family, group, or community, to be addressed with personal needs uppermost in mind, such as food, shelter, medical care, healing.

Betrayal adds other elements. Political considerations, for example. Katrina revealed official incompetence, callousness, and skewed priorities. Justice issues emerge, as the cleanup reveals inequitable distribution of concern and activity, not to mention goods and services. Systems that were supposed to work for all end up working for only a few.

The dismay and doubt caused by such betrayal do not dissipate once the crisis passes. They fester, and make people uncooperative and unwilling to sacrifice for a common good. The common good doesn't work for me, so why should I sacrifice for it?

Betrayal catches normal caregivers off guard. It doesn't fit our world of being nice and generous.

How do we deal with betrayal? If we are going to deal with the normal suffering of life, and the occasional big storm, we need to figure that out.

Betrayal, of course, is a central biblical theme, starting with Adam and Eve, Cain and Abel, Jacob and Esau, on to Judas Iscariot. Let's look at two betrayal stories: David's adultery with Bathsheba (2 Samuel 11—12), and Peter's betrayal of Jesus (Matthew 26:69-75, Mark 14:66-72).

King David saw Bathsheba bathing and sent for her. He lay with her, and she became pregnant. To save himself, David sent for Bathsheba's husband, Uriah the Hittite, and tried to maneuver him into sleeping with Bathsheba, so that he would think the child his. When that failed, David sent loyal Uriah into battle, and ordered his commander to abandon Uriah to certain death. David then took Bathsheba as his wife, and she bore a son.

Such is the face of betrayal. Abusing power and trust to satisfy one's desires, to promote personal interests, and to protect one's safety.

Betrayal wore a similar face when Simon Peter pretended not to know Jesus and denied him after Jesus' arrest. He had wanted to stand firm for Jesus, but when faced with danger, he saved himself.

These stories suggest three steps in dealing with betrayal.

The first step is to name it. David didn't get away with his perfidy. God sent the prophet Nathan to expose the King. "You are the man!" said Nathan. Similarly, Jesus named Peter's betrayal before it happened. There would be no hiding from the truth.

The second step is to experience consequences. God had more than an exposé in mind for David. From this day forth, the king would have great trouble in his household. He and Bathsheba would lose their son. Similarly, Simon Peter had the horrible experience of looking into Jesus' eyes after his master saw the betrayal. Peter wept bitterly.

The third step is to forgive. When David confessed his sin, Nathan said to him, "Now the Lord has put away your sin; you shall not die." David continued as king and continued to enjoy God's favor. Peter went on to become the disciples' leader and first spokesman.

How does that apply to our suffering?

I think we tend to explain suffering as bad luck, our own fault, or an isolated instance of someone else's bad behavior. All are true in some circumstances. Less true, but no less persuasive, is blaming our suffering on God.

To understand our world and its darkest moments, we need to recognize when suffering stems from betrayal, and then name it. The agony of economic dislocation, for example, might be something other than normal market forces. We need to see and to name perfidy, such as that for which Enron executives were convicted, and the less criminal, but no less disastrous, patterns of selfish management that grossly pad executive salaries while squandering workers' pensions.

It is fine to ask faith communities to fill in for government in providing relief. Churches need the mission work, and people will benefit. But when government is systematically abandoning the many in order to serve the few, we need to name the betrayal. For as we saw in Katrina, not even extraordinary outpourings of faith-community effort can rebuild a city that has been allowed, over many decades, to die.

Once we name the betrayal, we need to deal with the consequences. This will take us directly into the political realm, for failed social systems are generally a consequence of inept and/or corrupt leadership. In a sense, an electorate that pays scant attention to politics, especially at the nuts-and-bolts level, gets what it deserves. If we don't demand better from our leaders, why are we surprised when they let us down? Even if we didn't make the cruel and self-serving decisions that caused our suffering, we allowed the stage to be set.

Consequences require diligent follow-through. The cronies who eviscerated Enron must be held to account. The politicians who betray their office must be held accountable on Election Day. We cannot just shrug it off and resume our normal pursuits. Betrayal changes things.

Finally, forgiveness. As Christians, we don't have the luxury of endless retaliation. Jesus rewrote that law. Once betrayal is named and consequences are experienced, we need to move on. The classic example is divorce. Some marriages break up after betrayal, such as adultery or abuse. The wounded partner can carry that grudge forever. Better, I think, to let it go, move on, forgive oneself for having been a victim, forgive the other for being weak or mean. Better to forgive as Jesus taught us, and as he forgave Peter when he betrayed him.

Most of us will experience betrayal in some form or another. It will hurt us. It will diminish us. We can overcome the sting of it, however, if we are thoughtful, engaged, and committed to seeking reconciliation.

The aftermath of life's storms can be better days if we allow better days to occur.

Precious and Non-replaceable

Rowan Williams

This sermon was delivered at St. Paul's Cathedral, London, on November 1, 2005, at a service of remembrance for the victims of the London bombings of July 7, 2005. Printed with permission.

THERE is one thing that is always common to any sort of terrorist action, wherever it happens and whoever performs it. It aims at death—not the death of anyone in particular, just death. It does not matter to the killers if their victims are Jewish or Christian or Muslim, Hindu or Humanist; what matters is that they show that they can kill where they please.

And the shock of terrorist violence is just this sense of arbitrariness. It really doesn't matter who you are, what you have done or not done, what you think and believe, you are still a target just by being where you are at a particular time. The terrorist is the enemy not just of a system or a government but of the whole idea that we are each of us unique and responsible and non-replaceable. If it were true that one victim would be as good as any other, which is what the terrorist believes, the human world would be a completely different place, unrecognizable to most of us.

We are here grieving, after all, because those who so pointlessly and terribly died were, each one of them, precious, non-replaceable. And those who suffered injury and deep trauma and loss are likewise unique, their minds and hearts scarred by this suffering. Time gives perspective and may bring healing; but the trauma of violence, and even more the death of someone we love, makes a difference that nothing will ever completely unmake. The poet W. H. Auden captures this sense of injuries that never really heal as he writes of the biblical story of the Massacre of the Innocents:

> *Somewhere in these unending wastes of*
> *delirium is a lost child, speaking of Long Ago*
> > *in the language of wounds.*
> *Tomorrow, perhaps, he will come to himself*
> > *in Heaven.*
> *But here Grief turns her silence, neither in*
> > *this direction,*
> > *nor in that, nor for any reason.*
> *And her coldness now is on the earth forever.**

The loss by violence of a loved person leaves always that chill, that silence. We know there really is a tomorrow; religious believers are confident that there is a "last awakening" to the face of God. But how very weak and trivial a thing our human love would be if the "language of wounds" did not haunt us, speaking of a unique face and voice and personality.

But that is why even our grief on an occasion like today becomes an action that is prophetic, challenging, an action that resists terror. To those who proclaim by their actions that it doesn't matter who suffers, who dies, we say in our mourning, "No. There are no generalities for us, no anonymous and interchangeable people. We live by loving what's special, unique in each person. Everyone matters."

---

* W. H. Auden, *For the Time Being: A Christmas Oratorio*, 1945.

It is the vision that Jesus spells out in his words in Luke's gospel: the sparrows in the streets are two a penny, yet not one of them is forgotten by God. Every life is a special sort of gift. When we behave as if that were true, we do what's most important for the defeat of terror and indiscriminate violence. We want to live and work as though each person mattered; as if we did indeed believe in a love that forgot nothing and no one.

So that whatever else we do in response to terror, we need both to grieve honestly and to renew our commitment to a society and a morality that will take seriously the uniqueness of each person. And there is another thing worth remembering—something true of every bereavement but true in a special way here. Those we have lost are alive in and with God; but there is a sense in which they are alive in us too. Their unique existence has made us more profoundly who we ourselves are; and what they have given us by being themselves is part of the resource we now have to cope with the tragedy of their loss.

You've heard people say at times, I'm sure, that someone they've lost feels very close to them, encouraging them to carry on, to let go a little. It's a deeply important part of the process of healing that has to go on after a death—and it is something that is in part made possible by the person we have lost, by what they have contributed to our lives. It says to us that as we slowly begin the long and hard task of returning to a life without someone we love, this doesn't mean that we forget them or that our love is less—it is that this is part of how they live in us and how their love for us continues.

I wonder if we can let them help us not only with our loss but also with our fear? Because there is no denying that after a dreadful act of violence we feel fear as well as grief;

and the last few months have seen many people trying to respond to this widespread fear, trying to calm and assure us. One reaction is through security provision and new legislation. Another has been in the powerful and consistent responses of all our faith communities. As it happens, this commemoration falls at a time when several of us are marking or approaching significant festivals in our religious calendars. So we face the tragedy together today, drawing on our most important resources.

When we are aware of a deep bond with the departed, it sometimes helps us see that death in itself is not the thing most to be feared. We acknowledge the awful hurt of bereavement, especially of violent bereavement. Yet we have some abiding sense that death, even violent and untimely death, cannot destroy our relationships at the most important level; that love is indeed, as the Bible says, strong as death.

No, it is not death itself that should be the focus of fear. Rather, we should be afraid of losing just that passionate conviction about the beauty and dignity of each unique person that brings us here today. We should be afraid of losing the thing that, above all else, sets faith, humanity, civilization apart from the mind and the world of the terrorist. Jesus tells us not to fear those who can destroy the body, but those who can destroy body and soul; and part of the sickness of spirit we feel when confronted with terrorism is that we face people whose souls are damaged, almost destroyed.

It shows us what we can rightly fear—a world, a mind, caught up in terrible untruth, in a rejection of God's creation of diversity and unique beauty. To say that this is a tragic and pitiable fate is not at all to take away from the condemnation that terrorist violence deserves.

But today is not an occasion for us to focus on fear. What most matters is that we celebrate two things. First and most simply, we celebrate those we love, whose lives have been terribly damaged, and especially those whose lives have been cut short—but who are remembered in their separate, unique beauty, who remain with us and in us, and who are infinitely precious to God our creator and redeemer. Second, we give thanks that we live in a climate where the value and dignity of each person is still taken for granted; and we renew our resolution not to let this heritage be cheapened or abandoned in any way. God does not forget the smallest of his creatures. And he calls us all to share that loving, sometimes painful, remembering by which we honor the gifts given us through the lives of our dear friends, parents and children, sisters and brothers. There is silence in grief, as the poet reminded us; but there are still words in our hearts, images, and thoughts, which cannot be destroyed and which today we hold before God, praying that we may all, with those we love, "come to ourselves" in heaven.

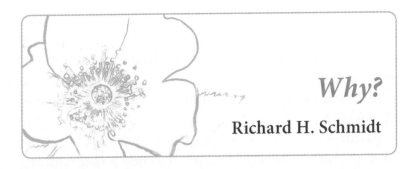

Why?

Richard H. Schmidt

DEATH itself is not the tragedy. Death is a good and natural thing, and the Bible often refers to it in benign terms such as being "gathered to our fathers." On one memorable day in 1999 I buried two parishioners, aged ninety-three and ninety-one. Both funerals were occasions for celebration rather than for sadness. Each woman had been a pioneer of a sort, exercising leadership in the church at a time when few women were admitted to leadership positions. Each had enjoyed a full and fruitful life and grown frail in her old age. Neither had been afraid to die. Both had been ready, even eager, for their "entrance into the land of light and joy." Testimonies of loving friends and well-wishers marked their departures from this life. These were holy deaths, and if there were tears, they were tears of thanksgiving.

Death is part of God's plan. The fact that we die keeps life from becoming an empty exercise of motion without meaning. If there were no death, we could bring no children into the world. The same fixed number of souls would live from aeon to aeon, neither growing nor dying nor giving birth, never older, never wiser. There would be nothing to accomplish or discover or conquer or experience for the first time, no mountains to climb, no risks to take, no choices to make, no hope of heaven, no fear of hell. We would soon cease to possess functioning souls and become listless, mindless bodies drifting endlessly about. Life would be rooted in no reality beyond what could be seen outside any window.

Our problem with death is not with death itself, but with particular deaths. On October 31, 1973, ordained just three years, I was beginning my third week as priest in charge of St. John's Church in Charleston, West Virginia, after the departure of the two senior priests who had supervised me until the month before. I had left the church that morning to see a friend when the phone rang. It was the church office calling to inform me that the daughter of a vestryman had been murdered the night before in a San Francisco parking lot by the Black Panther terrorist group, apparently a random slaying. The next several days were a blur for me, and probably for the family. I went with them to the funeral home to identify the sliced up body of their daughter and sister. I discussed the funeral with them, and then conducted the service. I spent hours in their home. Perhaps never in my life have I felt so inadequate. This was only my second funeral. What was I supposed to do? What could I say to these people? How could I assuage their loss? Comforting words did not come to me. I tried to think of something, anything to say, but everything that came to mind seemed like a cliché unworthy of the moment. So when I said anything, it was a passing comment on some idle topic like the weather or the food friends had brought to the house. Most of the time I sat with the family, tears rolling down my cheeks, saying nothing.

It is all very well to say that death is part of God's plan—but why does God allow my daughter to die at such a young age? Why with such pain and suffering? As a result of senseless violence? When she could still have contributed so much? When others loved and needed her? The deaths of children and teenagers were always the most difficult for me as a priest, and most difficult of all were teen suicides. I dealt with three teen suicides. What possible sense could there be to such a tragedy? What is there to say?

I shall never forget what the mother of the young woman murdered by the Black Panthers said to me after her daughter's funeral: "You will never know how much your words meant to us."

This expression of gratitude astonished me because I knew I had said nothing of any substance. Despite my theological education, I couldn't think coherently about such an event, much less speak coherently of it. I had felt embarrassed at my inability to say the right thing. What words could she possibly have meant? When I mentioned this later to an older, more experienced priest, he said the mother's remark didn't surprise him. "It doesn't matter what you say," he explained. "It's that you were there. Your presence and your tears were the best gift you could have given them. That's what they heard."

The right words are not necessary in times of tragedy, but the wrong words can make things worse. In dealing with people facing tragedy, I have learned to avoid pat answers, and when I hear them coming from the lips of others, I voice my disagreement. People often try to make mourners stop grieving, as if they should feel good about the tragic loss of a loved one. To grieve is natural, even essential, if healing is to come, and grief often includes anger, confusion, despondency, and doubt. This is true even for those with deep religious faith, and words that invalidate grief are not of God. One of the most honest and helpful books on this topic that I know of is C. S. Lewis's *A Grief Observed,* in which the great Christian teacher asks all the hard questions following the death of his wife and dismisses all the easy answers. Lewis does not flinch in the darkness.

"It's God's will," someone often says. That's rubbish. It is only God's will in that God allows a world in which tragedy can occur, but if God picks and chooses certain souls upon whom to inflict searing pain, then we should resist God, not serve him.

"God has taken her to be with him in heaven," someone else will say. More rubbish. A god who would choose to take someone away in the prime of life from those who love her because he wants her with him in heaven is a vicious god, and I refuse to serve him.

"This is part of God's grand plan which we cannot know," someone else will say. Not quite rubbish. I believe God does have a grand plan and that God is able to take a human tragedy and work it into his plan (the crucifixion of Jesus is the best example of that), but God's plan doesn't include his arbitrarily torturing selected persons. What do these people mean when they speak of God's grand plan? Do they envision their God sitting on his heavenly throne and saying, "Sam, you get fired today. Henry, you win the lottery. A healthy baby for Alice, a sick baby for Hazel. Sandra, a hurricane blows your house away today, and for you, Bob, a fatal car crash"? No, if that's the kind of god you believe in, keep him to yourself; I want no part of him.

I eventually found some things to say in the face of tragedy that are a cut above such drivel, but they address tragedy only on the intellectual level and they don't make us feel better when the pain is specific and our own. It's easy to theorize why God might allow pain and tragedy. A world with no pain would be no better than a world with no death. A car traveling at high speed toward a ditch would stop whether or not the driver applied the brake; a killer's bullet would turn to jelly before striking its victim; a mountain climber losing his grip would drift harmlessly to the ground; a deadly virus would be rendered inert just as it enters your lungs. Such a world would have no laws of nature because nature would be forever adjusting her ways so as to inflict no pain. There would be no sciences because science requires enduring structures to investigate. In the absence of pain, there would be no need for generosity, forgiveness, kindness, sacrifice, loyalty, commitment, work, or love. That would be a very different world from the world God created. I suppose God placed us in this world because human beings are not "finished" creatures, but rough models which require growth and refining, and God knew the kind of environment in which the growth and refining we need could take place. So there is tragedy in the world, and there is injustice, want, sorrow, death—boundless opportunities for generosity, forgiveness, kindness, and the like. This is an intellectual answer to the problem of pain. Some people find it satisfactory, as an intellectual exercise, but it doesn't help when your daughter is murdered.

Even this explanation does not fully address the problem of pain. What about pain intentionally inflicted by one person on another? Earthquakes and tornadoes are one thing, but why does God allow war, genocide, murders of innocent young women in parking lots, and the countless little acts of cruelty we inflict on one another every day? These evils are the consequences of decisions resulting from human freedom. Freedom is a gift, not a curse. God creates us for the purpose of entering into a relationship of love, obedience, and joy with him. He could have programmed us so that we would invariably adore him and follow his instructions, like robots or computers, but then we would not be free. For love, obedience, and joy to have meaning, they must be freely chosen, and that means the choice of hatred, disobedience, and misery is also open to us. Freedom is risky, but it's a risk

God decides to take every time a baby is born. God will not stop us, however destructively we may behave. He is willing to endure the consequences of our freedom in order to hold open the possibility of our love. I doubt this is any easier for God than it is for us. God honors us by saying to us, "*Thy* will be done; have it *your* way." Human freedom is God's will, of course—but not every act that results from it is God's will. This also is a merely intellectual answer, though, and it isn't worth a nickel when your daughter is murdered.

It has often been pointed out that in Christian thinking, not only does God not inflict pain and suffering on his people, but—and this is, so far as I know, a uniquely Christian understanding—God identifies with the suffering. This identifying is no mere sympathy from a distance, but an entering into the midst of human suffering and enduring the horror of it himself. Only Christians worship a bleeding, crucified God—the very idea of such a God is inconceivable or blasphemous to other faiths. What this means for Christians is that however grievous our life may be, God has walked this way before us. Pain, tragedy, death, and all the rest of it can be encounters with the divine. They can also, of course, induce despair and nihilism. It has to do, I think, with what you're looking for. Those who lack eyes to see God will not see him, even in a resplendent sunset, whereas those with eyes to see God will see him everywhere, even in the darkest dungeon.

Fourteenth century Europe was a bleak time. The Black Death was devastating the continent, wiping out as much as half the population in many areas, while the brutal and pointless Hundred Years War dragged on between France and England. The literature, theology, and art of the day contain dire warnings and visions of the torments of hell. It is remarkable that such a time could produce someone like Julian of Norwich. Julian spent fifty years in a small cell attached to a church in Norwich, England, giving counsel to those who sought her out and writing reflections on a series of sixteen visions of God she had received on the afternoon of May 13, 1373. The recurring theme is the goodness of God. Julian saw God's beauty, generosity, grace, and courtesy in every moment, every event, and every person. She wrote:

> ...there are many deeds which in our eyes are so evilly done and lead to such great harms that it seems to us impossible that any good result could ever come of them.... And the cause is this: that the reason which we use is now so blind, so abject and so stupid that we cannot recognize God's exalted, wonderful wisdom, or the power and the goodness of the blessed Trinity.

In perhaps the best known of her reflections, Julian wrote, "And so our good Lord answered all the questions and doubts which I could raise, saying most comfortingly: I may make all things well, and I can make all things well, and I shall make all things well...and you will see yourself that every kind of thing will be well."

Nearly four hundred years later, Jean-Pierre de Caussade, a French Jesuit, wrote a series of letters to a group of nuns for whom he served as spiritual director. These were later collected into a volume called *Abandonment to Divine Providence* which has helped many who sought a glimpse of God under tragic circumstances. He wrote:

> No matter what troubles, unhappiness, worries, upsets, doubts and needs harass souls who have lost all confidence in their own powers, they can all be overcome by the

marvelous hidden and unknown power of the divine action. The more perplexing the situation, the more we can hope for a happy solution. The heart says, "All will be well. God has the matter in hand. We need fear nothing." Our very fear and sense of desolation are verses in this hymn of darkness. We delight in singing every syllable of them, knowing that all ends with the "Glory be to the Father."

In God's time, in God's way, God will sort out all things and make all things well. It is God, not we, who will do this—if the job of sorting things out and making things well were ours, we would botch it up. When my loved ones die— and when the time comes for me to die, if I am given time to consider my death and if I have my wits about me—I hope I shall rest securely in God's arms, allowing him to carry me to that place where sorrow and pain are no more. Then finally, when I've arrived and he's seen me settled in, I hope God will grant me a few minutes one-on-one—because I have some questions.

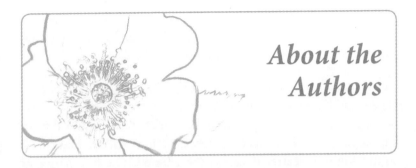

About the Authors

David J. Bena retired in 2006 as bishop suffragan of Albany in New York. He previously served parishes in North Carolina, Texas, and New York and as the executive assistant to the bishop of the Armed Forces. He is author of *Your Faith: Memorial, Memory, Miracle* (Forward Movement, 2003).

Thomas L. Ehrich is a priest, writer, and retreat leader living in Durham, North Carolina. He has served parishes in Indiana, Missouri, and North Carolina and writes *On a Journey,* an online daily devotional magazine. He is author of *With Scripture As My Compass: Meditations for the Journey* (Abingdon, 2004) and *Just Wondering, Jesus: 100 Questions People Want to Ask* (Morehouse, 2005).

Kathryn Greene-McCreight is a Connecticut native now serving as a parish priest in New Haven, Connecticut. She is author of *Feminist Reconstructions of Christian Doctrines* (Oxford University Press, 2000) and *Darkness Is My Only Companion: A Christian Response to Mental Illness* (Brazos, 2006), from which "The Light Shines in the Darkness" is adapted. She is now writing a commentary on Galatians for the *Brazos Theological Commentary on the Bible.*

Robert Horine has served as a staff writer at Forward Movement and as a reporter, editor, and priest. Influenced by Frederick Buechner, Garrison Keillor, and the strong storytelling tradition of his native Kentucky, he writes about people's connectedness to God and one another. His articles have appeared in several periodicals. He lives in Lexington, Kentucky.

Lee Krug, a psychotherapist and couples counselor, lives in New Jersey and has written for *Forward Day by Day*. She has led personal growth and study groups in her parish. She is married to an Episcopal priest and together they have four children and nine grandchildren, scattered across the country. She is a native of Chattanooga, Tennessee.

Carol McCrea, Ph.D. is a clinical psychologist in private practice in New Jersey. A former instructor in Medieval Literature, Carol is a widow and the mother of two adult children. She is a parishioner of St. James Memorial Episcopal Church, Eatontown, New Jersey.

Edward J. Mills III is rector of St. Paul's Church, Kingsport, Tennessee. A priest for over twenty-five years, he has served parishes in his native West Virginia and in Tennessee. He and his wife Karen are the parents of two grown children.

Gregory A. Russell is pastor of First Christian Church (Disciples of Christ) in Madison, Indiana. He has served previous pastorates in Kentucky, Indiana, and Ohio and is a trained interim ministry specialist. For nineteen years, he was married to Jane E. McAvoy, a theologian and church historian, who died suddenly in June 2004.

Frederick W. Schmidt is a priest serving as director of spiritual life and formation and associate professor of Christian spirituality at the Perkins School of Theology at Southern Methodist University in Dallas, Texas. He is author of *A Still Small Voice: Women, Ordination, and the Church* (Syracuse University Press, 1998), *The Changing Face of God* (Morehouse, 2001), *Conversations with Scripture: Revelation* (Morehouse, 2005), and *What God Wants for Your Life* (HarperSanFrancisco, 2005).

Richard H. Schmidt is editor and director of Forward Movement, Cincinnati, Ohio. A native Kentuckian, he is a priest who has served parishes in West Virginia, Missouri, and Alabama. His books include *Glorious Companions: Five Centuries of Anglican Spirituality* (Wm. B. Eerdmans, 2002), *Praises, Prayers, and Curses: Conversations with the Psalms* (Forward Movement, 2005), and *Life Lessons from Alpha to Omega* (Church Publishing, 2005), from which "Why?" is reprinted with permission.

John J. Thatamanil is assistant professor of theology at Vanderbilt Divinity School, Nashville, Tennessee. A native of India, he is author of *The Immanent Divine: A Hindu-Christian Conversation about God and the Human Predicament* (Fortress, 2006) and *Mission in the Marketplace: Metropolitan Chrysostom on the Identity and Mission of the Mar Thoma Church* (CSS Press, 2002). "Against Explanation and for Consolation" was originally published in *The Spire*, the alumni magazine of Vanderbilt Divinity School, and is reprinted with permission.

Desmond Tutu retired as archbishop of Cape Town, South Africa, in 1996. In 1984 he received the Nobel Peace Prize for his efforts to end apartheid in South Africa. He served as chair of South Africa's Truth and Reconciliation Commission from 1995 to 1998. A collection of his sermons, speeches, and incidental writings may be found in *The Rainbow People of God* (Image Books, 1994) and he is the author of *No Future Without Forgiveness* (Doubleday, 1999) about his work with the Truth and Reconciliation Commission. His latest book is *God Has a Dream: A Vision for Hope in Our Time* (Doubleday, 2004).

Francis H. Wade retired in 2005 after twenty-two years as rector of St. Alban's, Washington, D.C. He had previously served parishes in his native West Virginia. Wade has been a deputy to the General Convention of the Episcopal Church eleven times. He is author of *Jubilee People, Jubilee Lives* (Forward Movement, 2001), based on his meditations as chaplain to the House of Deputies in 2000, and of *The Art of Being Together* (Forward Movement, 2005). He is in demand as a retreat leader and speaker on parish ministry and the spiritual life.

Rowan Williams is archbishop of Canterbury. His books include *The Wound of Knowledge: Christian Spirituality from the New Testament to St. John of the Cross* (Darton, Longman and Todd, 1979), *Christ on Trial: How the Gospel Unsettles Our Judgement* (Fount, 2000), *On Christian Theology* (Blackwell, 2000), and *Writing in the Dust: Reflections on 11th September and its Aftermath* (Hodder and Stoughton, 2002).

Mary Wilson, a wife and mother of two adult children, is a life-long Roman Catholic and resident of New Richmond, Ohio. She resigned her job in the loan department of a bank in 2005 when she was unable to continue working because of amyotrophic lateral sclerosis (Lou Gehrig's disease), which had been diagnosed a year earlier, when Mary was forty-six.